# Birds of Portugal
## An Annotated Checklist

Gonçalo Elias

# Birds of Portugal
## An Annotated Checklist

| | |
|---|---|
| Title: | Birds of Portugal: An Annotated Checklist |
| Author: | Gonçalo Elias |
| Text revision: | Carlos Pacheco and Pedro Ramalho (original edition), Colm Moore (English edition) |
| Cover page: | Eurasian Scops Owl *Otus scops*(Pedro Marques) |
| Production: | C. Maria Elias |
| Printing: | Kindle Direct Publishing |
| Distribution: | Amazon.com |

3rd edition, March 2020

ISBN: 978-1658662222

Print On Demand

Contact: goncalo.elias@gmail.com

# CONTENTS

| | |
|---|---|
| Introduction | 7 |
| Methodology | 9 |
| List presentation | 12 |
| Part One: Wild Birds | 13 |
| Part Two: Birds of uncertain origin | 115 |
| Part Three: Non-native birds | 117 |
| Bibliography | 123 |
| Index | 127 |
| Glossary of place names | 139 |
| About the author | 149 |

# Introduction

In recent years birdwatching activities have markedly increased in Portugal, as a result of an increasing interest shown by society at large. This interest appears to be the result, on one hand, of a greater awareness being shown towards environmental issues and, on the other hand, of technological innovations, digital photography and the Internet amongst them, which made it easier to get and share pictures of the natural world, at low cost.

Thanks to this rapid increase in the number of people interested in birds, the amount of information about birds seen in the wild in Portugal has also risen sharply in the last few years. Because of that, existing references, namely those that deal with bird species occurring in Portugal and with their status in this country, become rapidly outdated.

*Birds of Portugal - An Annotated Checklist* has therefore been written with two objectives in mind. First, to provide an update to the existing species lists and second, to make this information available in a practical and accessible format that can be easily understood and used by anyone with an interest in birds, including those that belong to the non-specialized public.

The format chosen – an annotated list – is more than just an inventory: for each species mentioned, a brief description is provided about its migratory status, abundance and distribution in mainland Portugal. For the species that are only irregularly recorded – often referred to as 'rarities' – a brief summary of the existing records is provided.

This list is an update of the previous edition, which was published in 2017. The contents have been totally reviewed. Additionally, several species, which have been recorded in mainland Portugal for the first time during the last three years, have been added to the list. Several texts were also updated, in order to provide information about recent sightings. Furthermore, the taxonomy was updated according to the most recent international standards (please see Methodology).

The author hopes that this list will, in a modest way, contribute to a better understanding of the avifauna of mainland Portugal. This work will also be used as a basis for any future updates, whenever there is a relevant amount of new information to be added.

# Methodology

In order to construct this annotated bird list, all available information concerning birds that have been recorded in the wild in mainland Portugal has been consulted. In this section, the criteria used for selecting the information are presented.

Geographical span

This book focuses on the territory of mainland Portugal, as well as on the adjacent marine areas, which form the so-called Exclusive Economic Zone (EEZ).

The autonomous regions of the Azores and Madeira are to be the subject of a subsequent volume, as the bird life of these offshore archipelagos is rather different from that of the mainland. In this sense, if no other they deserve to be treated separately.

Time span

The list comprises available information about all the birds recorded in mainland Portugal up until the last day of December 2019.

Sources of information

All records that have been published in books, journals and other works were taken into consideration. Additionally, several recent records that have not been published on paper but that were made available via the Internet, namely in specialized sites, online databases, blogs and discussion groups, are included.

During the preparation of this list, many relevant works were checked. The most important ones are:

- *Aves de Portugal – Ornitologia do território continental*, for information about movements and distribution;

- *Atlas das Aves Nidificantes em Portugal*, for information about the distribution and abundance of breeding birds;

- *Portuguese Rarities Committee Reports*, for records of rare or vagrant species;

- *Anuário Ornitológico*, for data about the species of uncertain origin, for information about exotic birds and also for records of uncommon species;

- *Aves Exóticas que nidificam em Portugal Continental*, for information about the situation of non-native birds.

A full list of all works checked can be found in the Bibliography section (page 123).

## Validation of records

The identification of birds in the wild is not always easy and identification errors occur, often as a result of confusion with other species. In order to clarify the status of birds that turn up away from their normal distribution area, the information referring to rare birds is usually scrutinized by experienced members of a rarities committee. These committees produce reports relating to accepted records of rare birds. In the case of Portugal, this task was accomplished by the Iberian Rarities Committee (Comité Ibérico de Rarezas) between 1987 and 1994 and by the Portuguese Rarities Committee (Comité Português de Raridades or PRC) from 1995 onwards.

The most recent records (especially those made between 2013 and 2019) have not yet been included in any reports. However, in most cases, the birds were photographed and the pictures have been published on the Internet, namely in forums, blogs or photography groups. In many cases, the identification of the birds does not raise significant doubt, so it is reasonable to presume that these records will be accepted and hence they have been included in this list.

In the case of records dating from before 1987, the existing documentation is sometimes rather poor. In these cases, relevant published information has been included in the list, mentioning the quality of the existing evidence, where appropriate.

## Common Bird Names

Despite all the efforts carried out by different organizations to standardize common bird names, there are many species for which there can be more than one name, as there are extant many lists of names. This can be a source of confusion.

The common names used in this list are those used by the International Ornithologists' Union (IOU, formerly IOC), version 9.2.

## Scientific Bird Names

The systematics of birds has undergone changes in recent years, and there are varying arguments about what is the best taxonomic approach. The existing institutions and field guides use different criteria, and often this is also a source of confusion for birdwatchers.

In the present list, the sequence and the scientific names follow the recommendations of the IOU, version 9.2.

## List presentation

The following list comprises 494 species that have been seen in the wild in mainland Portugal.

The information about the species has been grouped as follows:

- Part One: Birds that have been recorded in an apparently natural state or which have wild self-sustaining populations – this includes autochthonous species, natural vagrants and exotic species that have naturalized themselves – 465 species.

- Part Two: Birds of uncertain origin – species that have been recorded, but for which their putative wild origin raises some doubts or cannot be ascertained – 7 species.

- Part Three: Non-native birds – species recorded in the wild as a result of introductions or escapes from captivity which have bred in the wild but for which no self-sustaining populations are known; it also includes species for which breeding is believed to have taken place – 22 species.

# Part One: Wild Birds

The list presented in this section comprises 465 species of birds that have been recorded in an apparently natural state or which have wild self-sustaining populations – this includes autochthonous species, natural vagrants and exotic species that have naturalized themselves.

1.  **Western Capercaillie** *Tetrao urogallus*

    Nowadays extinct, probably bred at Serra do Gerês and in the surrounding areas until the early part of the 20th century.

2.  **Red-legged Partridge** *Alectoris rufa*

    A common resident which can be found throughout the country in open or lightly wooded areas, both in the plains and in the highlands. It is more numerous inland than near the coastline, and it is particularly abundant in south-eastern Alentejo and north-eastern Algarve. In some areas, the wild populations are supplemented with released birds.

3.  **Grey Partridge** *Perdix perdix*

    Extirpated as a breeding species. It occurred in the northern highlands until the middle of the 20th century, or perhaps later, but it is now long gone. However, this species still occurs in neighbouring areas of Spain and stragglers may occur at times, such as the one shot in 2003 in the Serra de Montesinho. In January 2017, after a heavy snowstorm, a small flock was recorded with a camera trap at the same location.

### 4.C Common Quail *Coturnix coturnix*

A common and widespread breeding species, which is however scarce along the northern and central coastlines. It is particularly abundant in the Alentejo and in certain parts of the Trás-os-Montes province. This species is present in the country throughout the year, though its population is partially migratory.

### 5. Brant Goose *Branta bernicla*

A rare winter visitor, which has been recorded almost every year. At least 90 records are known. All sightings took place between September and mid-April, in coastal wetlands. Óbidos lagoon is the place where most sightings have been made. In the winters of 1991-92 and 2014-15, the species appeared in unusually large numbers, with sizeable flocks reported from various coastal locations.

### 6. Barnacle Goose *Branta leucopsis*

A rare and irregular winter visitor. At least 25 records are known, mostly between late November and mid-February, at coastal wetlands, but there is one record in the inner Alentejo. A maximum of six birds have been seen together.

### 7. Snow Goose *Anser caerulescens*

Only one record is known: a bird was seen in the Vila Franca de Xira plains in November 2019; it remained in the area until the end of the year. The origin of this bird is unclear and may be reassessed in the future.

### 8. Greylag Goose *Anser anser*

An uncommon winter visitor, which occurs from October through April. The main wintering site is the Tagus estuary, with smaller flocks recorded at the Sado estuary, Lagoa dos Patos (Alvito) and Alqueva reservoir. Occasionally recorded in other wetland areas in central and southern Portugal. In 2015, breeding was recorded at the Alqueva reservoir.

## 9. Taiga Bean Goose *Anser fabalis*

A very rare vagrant, with only a few records from early November to mid-February. Most sightings are from the Tagus estuary, with a single record from the Algarve. There are old reports of its presence in coastal central Portugal.

## 10. Pink-footed Goose *Anser brachyrhynchus*

Fifteen records are known to date: six in the Tagus estuary and the remaining ones at other coastal locations. Dates span from October to February.

## 11. Tundra Bean Goose *Anser serrirostris*

A very rare vagrant. There is a recent record, referring to a bird seen in the Vila Franca de Xira plains in November 2019. Additionally, it is possible that some previous records of Taiga Bean Goose actually refer to this species.

## 12. Greater White-fronted Goose *Anser albifrons*

A rare vagrant which has been recorded about eighteen times. Most sightings have involved singles or pairs, but on one occasion six birds were seen together and there is another sighting of four. Records took place between October and March, mainly in the Cávado, Mondego, Tagus and Sado estuaries, but there are two inland records in the Alentejo region. There is also an old record from the Porto area.

## 13. Tundra Swan *Cygnus columbianus*

A very rare vagrant. A single record is known: two birds in the Minho estuary during the winter of 1985-86.

## 14. Whooper Swan *Cygnus cygnus*

Four recent records, all between November and February, from the Minho estuary, the Peniche area, the eastern Alentejo and the eastern Algarve. Additionally, there is an old record from the Ave river mouth.

## 15. Egyptian Goose *Alopochen aegyptiaca*

An introduced resident. Since 2005 there has been a clear increase in the number of birds seen in the wild. Countless records exist throughout the country, referring both to isolated individuals and to flocks, which in some cases exceeded 100 birds. Most sightings were made in western Portugal and also in the inner Alentejo, but there are also several records from Beira Interior and Algarve. Breeding away from captivity has been recorded at several places.

## 16. Common Shelduck *Tadorna tadorna*

An uncommon resident, which occurs in the eastern Algarve, in the Tagus estuary and occasionally at other coastal wetlands. It is rather rare inland. There is also a wintering population.

## 17. Ruddy Shelduck *Tadorna ferruginea*

About 70 records are known from 1990 onwards. Sightings have been made at every month of the year. May have bred in the wild. The origin of these birds has been questioned and many of them have likely escaped from captivity.

## 18. Garganey *Spatula querquedula*

A scarce passage migrant, which turns up regularly from February to April and again from August to October, with scattered records from other months. More conspicuous during the pre-nuptial passage, when males show their colourful breeding plumage. Also an irregular breeding species, in very small numbers. Occasionally recorded in winter.

## 19. Blue-winged Teal *Spatula discors*

A rare vagrant, with 18 known records, most of which in the southern half of the country, especially in the Algarve. The period of observation spans mid-September to early April. It should be noted that this is the only species of Nearctic duck for which the number of records peaks in March.

## 20. Northern Shoveler *Spatula clypeata*

A common winter visitor, which occurs mainly from September to April. As with most dabbling ducks, the winter population is largely concentrated in coastal wetlands; small numbers occur inland. There are several records during spring and breeding has been proved in the Alentejo and Algarve provinces, in very small numbers.

## 21. Gadwall *Mareca strepera*

An uncommon resident and probably wintering species, it breeds in several places over southern Portugal, mainly in reservoirs. It is widespread in the Alentejo province, but it also breeds in the Algarve. In winter it is most numerous at coastal wetlands. Rather rare to the north of the River Tagus.

## 22. Eurasian Wigeon *Mareca penelope*

A common but rather localised winter visitor, which occurs mainly from October to March, with occasional records from other months. The wintering population is mostly concentrated in the large coastal wetlands, namely the Ria de Aveiro, the Tagus and Sado estuaries and the Ria Formosa. Small numbers are also found inland.

BIRDS OF PORTUGAL: AN ANNOTATED CHECKLIST

## 23. American Wigeon *Mareca americana*

There are 14 records of this Nearctic duck: half of them at the pond of Dunas de São Jacinto (Aveiro) and the remaining ones at other wetlands. Most records took place between November and March.

## 24.℃ Mallard *Anas platyrhynchos*

A common resident, which can be found throughout the year on any type of wetland. More numerous in the southern half of the country, namely in the Alentejo, in the Ribatejo and in the eastern Algarve. Large numbers concentrate at coastal wetlands during autumn and early winter. The wintering population is augmented by birds coming from central and northern Europe.

## 25.𝒰 Northern Pintail *Anas acuta*

An uncommon winter visitor, which occurs from November to March, with occasional records from other months. Largely concentrated at large coastal wetlands, particularly in the Sado estuary, where it can be locally abundant. Quite scarce inland.

## 26.℠ Eurasian Teal *Anas crecca*

An abundant winter visitor, which occurs from September to March. It can be found in most coastal wetlands. The largest concentrations occur in the Tagus and Sado estuaries, at the pond of the Dunas de São Jacinto reserve (Aveiro) and in the lower Mondego marshes. It is also common inland.

## 27. Green-winged Teal *Anas carolinensis*

A rare vagrant which has been recorded 24 times, always between late November and early April. All sightings refer to males. The two places with the largest number of records are the pond of Dunas de São Jacinto (Aveiro) and the Tagus estuary. Isolated records are known from other wetlands in the central and southern parts of the country.

## 28. Marbled Duck *Marmaronetta angustirostris*

A rare vagrant, with 30 recent records, most of them in the south. The Tagus estuary is the location with the largest number of sightings, but there are also records from the Beira Litoral, the Alentejo and the Algarve regions.

## 29.✔ Red-crested Pochard *Netta rufina*

An uncommon species in Portugal, which occurs mainly in the south. It breeds in the Tagus estuary and also at several places in the Alentejo and in the Algarve. It is rare to the north of the River Tagus. In autumn and winter, it tends to concentrate at certain places, particularly at the Santo André lagoon, where a few hundred birds gather at times.

## 30✔ Common Pochard *Aythya ferina*

An uncommon winter visitor, its numbers seem to fluctuate markedly from year to year. It can be found at coastal and inland waters, usually in small numbers, but flocks of many hundred birds are reported on occasion. A few pairs breed locally in the Ribatejo, in the Alentejo and at coastal locations in the central Algarve.

## 31. Ferruginous Duck *Aythya nyroca*

A rare winter visitor, which occurs mainly in the south, from October to March, although there are a few records from other months as well. The largest known gatherings involved 27 birds at Vilamoura in November 2012 and 41 at the same location in October 2015. Breeds irregularly in the Algarve.

### 32. Ring-necked Duck *Aythya collaris*

About 40 records are known of this Nearctic vagrant, largely concentrated in the period from November to March, with a peak in December. Records come mainly from coastal wetlands, Santo André lagoon being the location with the largest number of sightings. There are also a few inland records in the Alentejo.

### 33. Tufted Duck *Aythya fuligula*

An uncommon winter visitor, seen mainly from October to March. This diving duck turns up at coastal and inland waters, almost always in small numbers, but flocks of more than one hundred are sometimes seen. The wintering population is small and has declined in recent decades.

### 34. Greater Scaup *Aythya marila*

A rare winter visitor, which occurs between October and February at coastal wetlands and, occasionally, on inland reservoirs. Most known records involve single birds, although small flocks have been seen at times.

### 35. Lesser Scaup *Aythya affinis*

A very rare vagrant. There are about ten records of this species, all made at coastal wetlands from November to March. One of the records involved two males; all other records refer to singletons.

### 36. King Eider *Somateria spectabilis*

Only one record: a bird was present near Galé beach, Grândola from January to March 2019, together with a Common Eider.

## 37. Common Eider *Somateria mollissima*

A very rare vagrant, which has been irregularly reported in autumn and winter. The few existing records come from estuaries or from the open sea, along the coastline. Five of the fourteen known sightings were made in the Algarve.

## 38. Surf Scoter *Melanitta perspicillata*

Six records are known, all between late November and late March. Three of them took place in the Lisbon area, another one at the Sado estuary and the remaining two in the Algarve.

## 39. Velvet Scoter *Melanitta fusca*

A rare vagrant from northern Europe, mainly recorded between December and March in northern and central Portugal, either along the coast or in estuaries. In December 1997 the species was recorded almost simultaneously at three different locations, suggesting that there was an influx in that year. In December 2016 the number of sightings was also above average. In December 2019, a flock of seven was recorded near Esposende. The number of records has increased in recent years – this increase could be related to a stronger observation effort along the coasts of northern Portugal.

## 40. Common Scoter *Melanitta nigra*

A common winter visitor, which occurs mainly in the open sea, not far from the coastline. Occasionally it is recorded at coastal wetlands. It is more numerous along the coast of northern and central Portugal. The main period of occurrence spans from August to April, with occasional sightings at other times of the year.

## 41. Long-tailed Duck *Clangula hyemalis*

About 30 records are known of this duck, all at coastal wetlands. Sightings have been made at all times of the year, but three quarters took place between November and February.

## 42. Bufflehead *Bucephala albeola*

Two records are known: a female at Arrábidas, Sado estuary, in January and February 1993 and a male at Aldeia Nova, Vila Real de Santo António, between January and May 2016.

## 43. Common Goldeneye *Bucephala clangula*

Seven records, mostly between November and January, at several coastal locations: Ave river mouth, Peniche, Cape Raso and Tagus estuary.

## 44. Smew *Mergellus albellus*

One ancient record: a bird shot by hunters near Alcochete in December 1911.

## 45. Common Merganser *Mergus merganser*

A very rare vagrant, with less than ten known records, all made from November to February and almost all at coastal wetlands. There is a single record away from the coast: one at a reservoir in Beira Alta. The winter of 2010-2011 was exceptional, with four records at different locations – on one instance, three birds were seen together.

## 46. Red-breasted Merganser *Mergus serrator*

An uncommon winter visitor, which occurs mostly between November and March at coastal wetlands. The Sado estuary is the most important site for this species, with up to 350 birds present in certain winters. Sometimes the species is recorded at other coastal wetlands, in very small numbers. It is rare inland, with a handful of sightings made at reservoirs in the Beira Alta and Alentejo regions.

## 47. Ruddy Duck *Oxyura jamaicensis*

A rare vagrant. Although this duck is native to North America, it has been introduced in the United Kingdom and it is believed that birds seen in Portugal have originated from this introduced population, but it is also possible that some of them refer to escapes from captivity. There are about seventeen records, of which one at the Boquilobo marsh, three at Quinta do Lago (Loulé) and the remaining ones, all referring to the same individual, in the Alentejo province. All records involved single birds.

## 48. White-headed Duck *Oxyura leucocephala*

A rare vagrant from the Mediterranean. Twelve records are known, of which nine were in the Algarve, one at Lagoa dos Patos (Alvito), one in the Tagus estuary and one at the Boquilobo marsh. Most records refer to single birds, although two or three were seen together on some occasions. Half of the sightings were made in October and November, the remaining ones at other times of the year.

## 49√ Red-necked Nightjar *Caprimulgus ruficollis*

An uncommon summer visitor, which breeds over most of the so-called areas of Mediterranean influence; its distribution area comprises much of southern Portugal and also the eastern regions north of the River Tagus. It occurs from April to September.

### 50. European Nightjar *Caprimulgus europaeus*

An uncommon summer visitor which is widespread north of the River Tagus and rather scarce further south. Birds on migration are sometimes recorded away from known breeding areas, namely at coastal locations in the south. The main period of occurrence ranges from mid-April until October.

### 51. Chimney Swift *Chaetura pelagica*

Two records are known: one at Salgados lagoon, Silves, in October 1999 and another one at Sagres, Vila do Bispo, in September 2013.

### 52. Alpine Swift *Tachymarptis melba*

An uncommon and localised summer visitor which breeds on cliffs, both coastal and inland. Occasionally it can breed on human-made structures. It is also a scarce passage migrant. Its main period of occurrence ranges from March to October.

### 53. Common Swift *Apus apus*

A common summer visitor, which is usually present from March to October, with a few records during the wintering period. It occurs throughout the country and is more frequent north of the river Tagus. Large flocks pass through the country during migration periods.

### 54. Pallid Swift *Apus pallidus*

A common summer visitor. It is widespread as a breeding species, but its distribution area is largely discontinuous. It seems to be more frequent in the southern half of the country. It occurs mainly between March and September and is rarely recorded outside this period.

## 55. Little Swift *Apus affinis*

About 25 records are known, most of them south of the River Tagus. More than half of the sightings were made between mid-May and mid-June, whereas the remaining ones took place between March and November.

## 56. White-rumped Swift *Apus caffer*

A rare summer visitor, which arrives in May and leaves in September, although there are a few records outside the main period of occurrence. Most sightings are from the eastern Alentejo and the Algarve and breeding has been confirmed at several places in both regions and also in Beira Baixa and Beira Alta. Additionally, there are recent records in the northeastern province of Trás-os-Montes.

## 57. Great Bustard *Otis tarda*

An uncommon resident which occurs mainly in the inner Alentejo. Its stronghold lies in the Castro Verde plains, which hold about 90% of the Portuguese population. In other areas, notably in Beira Baixa and Alto Alentejo, it has become extirpated as a breeding bird. Outside the breeding season, Great Bustards sometimes turn up in other parts of the country, mostly during summer months, almost always in small numbers.

## 58. Little Bustard *Tetrax tetrax*

An uncommon resident, it occurs mainly in the eastern Alentejo, where it is widespread and locally common. Elsewhere it is rare and localised, although it can be found from Trás-os-Montes in the north to the Algarve in the south. Recent data suggests that its breeding population, which is largely resident, is declining fast, even at some of its strongholds, and that the species may have disappeared from the northeast. During the summer months, it undertakes dispersive movements and regularly turns up at some locations where it does not breed.

### 59.✔ Great Spotted Cuckoo *Clamator glandarius*

An uncommon summer visitor, which occurs mostly in inland areas and is scarce near the coast. It is an early migrant that arrives in late January or February and leaves in July, although there are a few records outside this period. This species is a parasite and lays its eggs in the nests of corvids, showing a preference for those of the Common Magpie.

### 60.𝒞 Common Cuckoo *Cuculus canorus*

A common summer visitor, which can be heard in the south from late February onwards and a few weeks later in the north. From late June onwards, males become silent and this cuckoo is then difficult to locate, although it is known to occur until September. Like the preceding species, it is a parasite – its victims are mainly the smaller passerines.

### 61. Pin-tailed Sandgrouse *Pterocles alchata*

A very rare resident, which occurs only in the eastern part of the Beira Baixa province, where about ten pairs breed. Only exceptionally seen elsewhere. This population might be declining and close to becoming extirpated.

### 62. Black-bellied Sandgrouse *Pterocles orientalis*

A rare resident with a discontinuous distribution, which occurs in eastern Alentejo and in certain areas of the Beira Baixa province, but in the latter province its population is very small. The distribution area of this sandgrouse in Portugal probably shrank during the 20th century. The national population is believed to be about 500 birds.

## 63. C Rock Dove *Columba livia*

A common and widespread resident. Domestic and feral populations can be found in most towns and villages, usually in close association with man. Small pockets of apparently wild birds still survive in places along the rocky coast and in certain areas of Trás-os-Montes and Beira Interior, but even here there are often individual birds showing marks of the domestic type.

## 64. U Stock Dove *Columba oenas*

A scarce breeder and an uncommon winter visitor. During the breeding season, it occurs mostly in the highlands of the northeast, with scattered inland records further south. Elsewhere it is a non-breeding visitor; it occurs on autumn passage along the coast and during the winter in the Alentejo and in the southern part of Beira Baixa, usually in small numbers.

## 65. £ Common Wood Pigeon *Columba palumbus*

A common resident and winter visitor. As a breeding bird, it is found over most of the country, although it is scarce in the southwest. In the winter, large flocks occur in the Alentejo and Beira Baixa provinces, often with thousands of birds involved. Migrating parties also appear near the coastline at times.

## 66. y European Turtle Dove *Streptopelia turtur*

This summer visitor occurs over most of the country, but its abundance varies markedly: it is quite common to the north of the River Tagus, especially in the northeast, and rather uncommon further south. It occurs regularly on migration, particularly along the coast. The national population of this dove has been declining for several decades.

## 67. Eurasian Collared Dove *Streptopelia decaocto*

Has colonised the country during the last quarter of the 20th century and is nowadays a widespread and common bird throughout the country, although it is rare in the highlands, above 1000m height. This resident species is more frequent near the coast than at inland sites.

## 68. Water Rail *Rallus aquaticus*

An uncommon resident, which occurs mainly in coastal wetlands and, locally, in inland waters.

## 69. Corn Crake *Crex crex*

A very rare passage migrant, which was probably more regular in the past. Only nine records are known during the last 30 years. All recent records were made during the last quarter of the year, at various locations in the western half of the country. Most records refer to birds that were shot or found dead.

## 70. Little Crake *Porzana parva*

There are about 20 records of this species, all referring to single birds or groups of up to three, mainly at coastal locations. There were two records in 2008 and 2009 during the post-nuptial passage (August and September); the remaining ones were all during the pre-nuptial passage (March to May).

## 71. Baillon's Crake *Porzana pusilla*

Probably bred in the past, but is currently very rare in the country. Over the last 30 years, there have been no more than eleven records, all referring to singletons, mainly in spring and, occasionally, in autumn and winter.

## 72. Spotted Crake *Porzana porzana*

A rare passage migrant, which may also overwinter. A few tens of records are known, most of them referring to birds seen during the pre-nuptial (February to April) and post-nuptial passage (September to November), but there are several winter records. Most sightings were made in coastal wetland areas in the centre and south; on rare occasions, the species has also been seen inland.

## 73. Sora *Porzana carolina*

A very rare vagrant, which has been recorded only once: an individual was seen at Silves in January 2017; it remained in the area for six weeks.

## 74. Western Swamphen *Porphyrio porphyrio*

A scarce resident, which occurs in wetland areas in the centre and south of Portugal. It is more frequent in the Algarve (where it can be locally common) than elsewhere. After having declined to less than five breeding pairs, the population has been increasing steadily and new areas have been colonised, including some inland reservoirs in the Alentejo. The region of lower Mondego was colonised following a reintroduction project that began in 1999, and from there the species expanded northwards and southwards.

## 75. Allen's Gallinule *Porphyrio alleni*

One at Ria de Alvor, Portimão, in April 1990 and another one at Penamacor in January 1992.

## 76. Purple Gallinule *Porphyrio martinica*

One at Monsanto, Lisboa, in November 2013. This record happened during a historic influx along the North

American east coast, and several other records were made in mainland Europe and in the Azores.

### 77. Common Moorhen *Gallinula chloropus*

A common and widespread resident, which is more numerous to the south of the river Tagus and also in coastal areas to the north of the same river. It is rather scarce in the northeast.

### 78. Red-knobbed Coot *Fulica cristata*

There are at least 70 sightings of single birds or small flocks, in most cases south of the river Tagus. Records have been made at all times of the year, but there are clearly more during autumn and winter months. Some birds were carrying neck-collars, which had been placed as part of a reintroduction program that has been taking place in southern Spain. In 2011 a Red-knobbed Coot bred with a Eurasian Coot in the Castro Verde area.

### 79. Eurasian Coot *Fulica atra*

An uncommon resident, which occurs mainly in reservoirs and coastal lagoons, sometimes also in fish ponds. It can be locally numerous, with gatherings of hundreds or even thousands of birds having been recorded on several occasions. It is practically absent from the highlands and is generally scarce in the northern third of the country.

### 80. American Coot *Fulica americana*

One at Ludo, Faro, in September 1992.

### 81. Common Crane *Grus grus*

An uncommon winter visitor which arrives in late October and leaves in early March. It occurs almost only in the eastern Alentejo. Very rarely reported elsewhere. Its wintering population comprises about 12 thousand individuals.

## 82. Little Grebe *Tachybaptus ruficollis*

A common resident, which can be found throughout the country, although its abundance varies markedly. It is more numerous in the Alentejo, Ribatejo and Beira Baixa provinces and also at certain places along the central west coast and in the Algarve.

## 83. Pied-billed Grebe *Podilymbus podiceps*

A very rare vagrant, which has been recorded on three occasions only. The first sighting involved a bird seen at the Cávado estuary in November and December 2014; the second one was of an individual at the Venda Nova reservoir, Montalegre, in October 2016; finally, a bird was found near Sesimbra in June 2017 and it remained in the area for several months.

## 84. Great Crested Grebe *Podiceps cristatus*

An uncommon resident, which favours medium-sized and large reservoirs, mainly inland. Rather scarce along the west coast, where it is seen mainly in autumn and winter at certain coastal wetlands. There is however a small resident population on the Algarve coast.

## 85. Horned Grebe *Podiceps auritus*

A very rare vagrant, with only nine recent records. All sightings were made between November and March at coastal wetlands and involved single birds.

## 86. Black-necked Grebe *Podiceps nigricollis*

A scarce winter visitor, which favours estuaries, saltpans, and coastal lagoons and occurs mainly from mid-August to April. The Sado estuary and the Castro Marim reserve are the two main wintering sites and each of them can hold up to 100 birds at times. Elsewhere the species turns up in small numbers. Rather rare inland. Bred near Montemor-o-Novo, Alentejo, in 2007.

## 87. Greater Flamingo *Phoenicopterus roseus*

A non-breeding visitor that can be seen throughout the year, mainly at coastal wetlands in central and southern Portugal. Occasionally seen inland. Although it is generally uncommon, it can be locally abundant, mainly in the Tagus and Sado estuaries and in the Castro Marim reserve. Isolated breeding attempts are known to have occurred in the Algarve.

## 88. Common Buttonquail *Turnix sylvaticus*

Probably it was common in Portugal during the 19th century, especially in the southern half, but its population declined sharply during the 20th century and presently it may be extinct.

## 89. Eurasian Stone-curlew *Burhinus oedicnemus*

An uncommon resident, which occurs mainly south of the River Tagus; locally it also occurs further north, mainly near the Spanish border. It is more numerous in the eastern Alentejo and in the eastern Algarve than elsewhere.

## 90. Eurasian Oystercatcher *Haematopus ostralegus*

A scarce but regular passage migrant and winter visitor. Almost exclusively found along the coastal strip, being very rare inland. The Sado estuary and the Ria Formosa are the two most important areas for this species. It occurs mainly from August to April, although a few immatures oversummer.

## 91. Black-winged Stilt *Himantopus himantopus*

Breeds mostly on most coastal wetlands in the centre and south, where it can be locally common, and also inland in small numbers. Its migratory pattern is complex, some populations are probably resident, while others are summer migrants and yet some other are passage migrants or possibly winter visitors. Back in 1990 the species wintered in the eastern Algarve only, but its wintering area has expanded since then and currently, it extends as far north as Aveiro.

## 92. Pied Avocet *Recurvirostra avosetta*

A locally common winter visitor, which is numerous in the Tagus and Sado estuaries, sometimes also in the Mondego one; it is scarce on other coastal wetlands. Inland records are infrequent and typically refer to birds on migration. Breeding has been recorded regularly in the eastern Algarve and sporadically in the Tagus and Sado estuaries. Its wintering population is usually present from September to March.

## 93. Northern Lapwing *Vanellus vanellus*

A regular winter visitor, which is common south of the River Tagus and uncommon further north. It can be seen mainly from July to March, and it is particularly abundant from October to February. Breeding has been confirmed in several places in the central and southern parts of the country, but these events seem to be sporadic and nowhere regular.

## 94. Sociable Lapwing *Vanellus gregarius*

A rare vagrant which turns up irregularly during the winter period. About fifteen records are known, from early October to early March, all involving single birds seen at various places in southern Portugal. The Tagus estuary is the place with the highest number of records.

## 95 ~~C~~ European Golden Plover *Pluvialis apricaria*

A common winter visitor to the south which is however uncommon to the north of the River Tagus. It is patchily distributed, although it can be locally numerous. Often associates with flocks of Lapwings. Its main period of occurrence spans from October to February, but there are scattered records of isolated birds or small flocks at other times of the year.

## 96. Pacific Golden Plover *Pluvialis fulva*

One at the Tagus estuary in August 2005 and another one at Salgados lagoon, Silves, in July 2007.

## 97. American Golden Plover *Pluvialis dominica*

A rare vagrant from North America, which has been recorded on 40 occasions, chiefly in autumn. Most records were made close to the coast in the centre and south regions, but there are also three records from coastal areas in the north and two records inland. The two places with the highest number of records are the Tagus estuary and the Salgados lagoon, Silves.

## 98 ᴜ Grey Plover *Pluvialis squatarola*

An uncommon but regular non-breeding visitor. It occurs mainly in the large coastal wetlands, where it can be locally common at certain times of the year. Can also be seen in small numbers on beaches, but it is very rare inland. Mostly seen in winter and during passage periods; however, a few non-breeders remain in Portugal during the breeding season.

## 99. Common Ringed Plover *Charadrius hiaticula*

A common migrant and winter visitor, which can be seen in coastal wetlands and sometimes around inland waters. It is numerous during winter and also during passage periods, especially on post-nuptial passage, which peaks in August and September. Several birds remain in the country during the breeding season but do not breed.

## 100. Little Ringed Plover *Charadrius dubius*

Breeds throughout the country but is generally uncommon. It is more frequent in the south, especially in the eastern parts of Baixo Alentejo and Algarve, whereas to the north of the Tagus it is scarce and shows a patchy distribution. Mainly a summer visitor, occurring from March to September, but there are several winter records in the south.

## 101. Killdeer *Charadrius vociferus*

One at Azambuja in February 1998.

## 102. Kentish Plover *Charadrius alexandrinus*

A common resident and passage migrant, which can be found along the entire coastline, from Minho to Algarve. It can be locally numerous on migration, especially in large wetlands. This plover can also be found in the inner Alentejo in very small numbers; its breeding has been confirmed in the Alqueva reservoir.

## 103. Lesser Sand Plover *Charadrius mongolus*

One at the Sado estuary in August 2003.

## 104. Eurasian Dotterel *Charadrius morinellus*

A regular but very scarce passage migrant, which has been recorded only during the post-nuptial passage and, exceptionally, in winter. The place with the largest number of records is Cape St. Vincent, where the species has been seen almost every year, with small flocks turning up in September and October. Occasionally seen in other places along the coast and, rarely, inland.

## 105. Upland Sandpiper *Bartramia longicauda*

Four known records; the oldest involved a bird at Leça da Palmeira, Matosinhos, in February 1932; more recently, there are two records in the Algarve: one in September 1999 and another one in September and October 2010. The last record involved a bird on nocturnal migration near Sintra, in September 2011.

## 106. Eurasian Whimbrel *Numenius phaeopus*

An uncommon passage migrant and winter visitor, which is most frequently seen in coastal wetlands and rocky stretches of coastline close to the seashore. Spring passage is mostly in April and May, whereas autumn passage occurs from August to October. The small wintering population is largely concentrated in the south.

## 107. Hudsonian Whimbrel *Numenius hudsonicus*

A very rare vagrant. Three records of single birds are known from Óbidos lagoon. These records took place in three consecutive winters, so they might actually refer to the same returning individual.

## 108. Slender-billed Curlew *Numenius tenuirostris*

There is an old record of a bird caught in the Ribatejo province in the 19th century. This bird was kept in the

Bocage Museum of the Lisbon University until 1978 when the museum was destroyed by a fire.

## 109. Eurasian Curlew *Numenius arquata*

An uncommon non-breeding visitor, which is only regular in the large coastal wetlands; rather rare at small wetlands or away from the coast. Its main period of occurrence ranges from August to March, although there are a few records from other months.

## 110. Bar-tailed Godwit *Limosa lapponica*

A passage migrant and winter visitor which is generally uncommon; it is most often found in the large coastal wetlands, where it can be locally numerous; sometimes it can also be found in small numbers in other places along the coast, particularly on migration. It is rare inland. A few non-breeders remain in the country throughout the breeding season.

## 111. Black-tailed Godwit *Limosa limosa*

A common passage migrant and winter visitor, which occurs mainly in the large coastal wetlands and flooded areas; can also be found inland, albeit in smaller numbers. It is more abundant during migration periods; the pre-nuptial passage peaks in January and February, while the post-nuptial goes from July to October.

## 112. Ruddy Turnstone *Arenaria interpres*

A common passage migrant and winter visitor which can be found along the entire coastline and, more rarely, inland. It is present in the country mainly from August to May but is occasionally recorded during the breeding season.

## 113. Red Knot *Calidris canutus*

A scarce but regular migrant and winter visitor, which occurs mainly along the coast, where it can be numerous during the pre-nuptial passage, especially during the first two weeks of May. Very rare inland.

## 114. Ruff *Calidris pugnax*

ν An uncommon passage migrant and winter visitor. It usually occurs in wetlands and is thus more frequent along the coastline, but sometimes it turns up at inland sites. More numerous on passage, both pre-nuptial and post-nuptial, however, a few birds overwinter, especially in the south.

## 115. Broad-billed Sandpiper *Calidris falcinellus*

A very rare vagrant. There are seven records, all relating to single birds and all in coastal wetlands, from north to south. Sightings took place at different times of the year.

## 116. Sharp-tailed Sandpiper *Calidris acuminata*

One adult at Ria de Aveiro in March 2007.

## 117. Stilt Sandpiper *Calidris himantopus*

One at the Mondego estuary in October 2011.

## 118. Curlew Sandpiper *Calidris ferruginea*

υ An uncommon passage migrant and rare winter visitor. It occurs at most coastal wetlands, sometimes also inland, during the post-breeding migration, namely from August to October. Small numbers can also be seen during the pre-nuptial migration, especially in April and May, but there are records during other months as well. A small population comprising a few tens of birds may winter in Portugal.

### 119. Temminck's Stint *Calidris temminckii*

A rare passage migrant which may occasionally overwinter. A few tens of records are known, most of them south of the River Tagus. The species has been recorded at different times of the year but seems to be more frequent between August and March, with a peak in October.

### 120. Sanderling *Calidris alba*
*C*

A common passage migrant and winter visitor which can be seen along the coast, mainly on sandy or rocky beaches, but also in estuaries, saltpans and lagoons. Rather rare inland. It occurs almost throughout the year and is more numerous from August to early May.

### 121. Dunlin *Calidris alpina*
*C*

A common non-breeding visitor, which occurs mostly at coastal wetlands and is occasionally seen inland. It is more numerous in the large estuaries, especially during passage and winter times, but a few non-breeding individuals remain in the country throughout late spring and early summer.

### 122. Purple Sandpiper *Calidris maritima*

A rare winter visitor. It can be found in small numbers along the coastline, mostly in sectors with rocky beaches and also in breakwaters near harbours or river mouths.

### 123. Baird's Sandpiper *Calidris bairdii*

One at Ludo, Faro, in December 2004 and another one at Foz do Sizandro, Torres Vedras, in October 2019.

## 124. Little Stint *Calidris minuta*

ᑕ A regular non-breeding visitor, usually in small numbers, although large flocks occur at times. Like most sandpipers, it occurs almost only along the coastline, mainly in estuaries and coastal lagoons. Rare in inland waters. More frequent on passage periods and in winter, it is very scarce during late spring and early summer.

## 125. White-rumped Sandpiper *Calidris fuscicollis*

Eight records are known, all but one referring to single birds seen in October or November at coastal wetlands. During the autumn of 2013, three different birds were seen in just ten days.

## 126. Buff-breasted Sandpiper *Calidris subruficollis*

A rare vagrant, which has been recorded on 24 occasions. Apart from a bird seen in a reservoir in Trás-os-Montes, all records are from coastal locations and all but two refer to single birds. Most records took place between August and October, with a peak in September.

## 127. Pectoral Sandpiper *Calidris melanotos*

About 60 records are known, the majority of them in August, September and October, involving singletons or small parties of up to three birds. Most records are from coastal wetlands, but there are a few sightings from inland locations.

## 128. Semipalmated Sandpiper *Calidris pusilla*

Has been recorded six times. All records refer to single birds, seen at coastal locations between July and October.

## 129. Long-billed Dowitcher *Limnodromus scolopaceus*

About 20 records exist, mostly from wetlands in southern Portugal, both coastal and inland. There were two sightings of two birds and one of three, all the other ones refer to singletons. Records were made at various times of the year. The Tagus estuary is the place with most records.

## 130. Eurasian Woodcock *Scolopax rusticola*
*✓*

An uncommon winter visitor, for which little is known about the distribution and population, due to its shy habits. Probably occurs throughout the country, mostly from October to March.

## 131. Jack Snipe *Lymnocryptes minimus*

*✓* An uncommon winter visitor, which occurs throughout the country, especially in flooded areas, however, it is quite rare inland to the north of the River Tagus. It is present mainly from September to March, with very few records during other months.

## 132. Great Snipe *Gallinago media*

Three records are known, all of single birds: the first near São Cristóvão, Montemor-o-Novo, in February 1997, and the other two at the Tagus estuary, in 2003 and 2004, respectively.

## 133. Common Snipe *Gallinago gallinago*
*✓*

A common and widespread non-breeding visitor, which is most numerous in coastal lowlands, especially in flooded areas. It can be seen mainly from August to April. A small breeding population is known from the extreme north, namely at Serra do Gerês and in the nearby region of Barroso, however, this population underwent a sharp decline over the last decades and might be close to extirpation.

### 134. Wilson's Snipe *Gallinago delicata*

One shot in the plains of Lezíria Norte, Vila Franca de Xira, in December 2006.

### 135. Terek Sandpiper *Xenus cinereus*

Has been recorded seven times, three in the Tagus estuary, one in the Sado estuary and three in the Algarve. All records refer to single birds and were made from April to November, but the bird seen at the Sado estuary in 2019 remained during the wintering period.

### 136. Wilson's Phalarope *Phalaropus tricolor*

A very rare vagrant, which has been recorded on nine occasions at several coastal wetlands in central and southern Portugal. On one instance, a bird apparently overwintered at the Ilha da Morraceira saltpans, Figueira da Foz, from November 2010 until March 2011.

### 137. Red-necked Phalarope *Phalaropus lobatus*

About 45 records are known of this phalarope, almost all of them at coastal wetlands. Half of the sightings were made in the period ranging from August to October, but there are records for every month.

### 138. Red Phalarope *Phalaropus fulicarius*

A rare passage migrant and winter visitor, which is probably frequent offshore, but which rarely approaches the coast, therefore there are very few records away from the pelagic environment – the majority of these records were made after storms when birds were seen in coastal wetlands. Exceptionally it has been recorded inland. The period of occurrence ranges from August to March.

## 139. Common Sandpiper *Actitis hypoleucos*

✓ An uncommon species which can be found throughout the year, usually in small numbers. It is not clear whether the breeding individuals are resident. In spring, this wader occurs throughout the country in low densities but is more frequent in the eastern half. Outside the breeding season, it is also regularly seen near the coast, mainly near wetlands, both on passage and in winter.

## 140. Spotted Sandpiper *Actitis macularius*

Six records, all referring to single birds seen at different locations in central and southern Portugal. Most records took place in August and September.

## 141. Green Sandpiper *Tringa ochropus*

✓ An uncommon passage migrant and winter visitor which can usually be seen from January to March and again from late June until the end of the year, but there are a few spring records as well. It occurs throughout the country.

## 142. Solitary Sandpiper *Tringa solitaria*

One at Ria de Alvor, Portimão, in June 1989.

## 143. Lesser Yellowlegs *Tringa flavipes*

A rare vagrant, with about 50 records, half of them during the last quarter of the year. Almost all sightings refer to single birds, but on one occasion two birds were seen together; most records were made at coastal wetlands in central and southern Portugal.

### 144. Willet *Tringa semipalmata*

One at the Ribeira das Enguias saltpans, near Alcochete, in April 2009.

### 145. Common Redshank *Tringa totanus*

A common passage migrant and winter visitor, which occurs in all large and medium-sized coastal wetlands. Very rare inland. It can be seen throughout the year, although it is scarce during the breeding season. Has bred occasionally in very small numbers at a few coastal wetlands in central and southern Portugal.

### 146. Marsh Sandpiper *Tringa stagnatilis*

A rare passage migrant, with about 45 known records, all referring to single birds seen mainly in the Tagus and Sado estuaries or in the Algarve, with a few sightings along the coasts of central Portugal. The summer months account for about two thirds of the existing records.

### 147. Wood Sandpiper *Tringa glareola*

A scarce passage migrant, which occurs mainly between February and April and again between August and October; occasionally it is recorded at other times of the year, even in winter, albeit in very small numbers. Largely found in coastal wetlands, but sporadically recorded inland.

### 148. Spotted Redshank *Tringa erythropus*

A regular but scarce non-breeding visitor, which occurs in coastal wetlands and, more rarely, inland. It is not infrequent on passage, both in spring and autumn; additionally, a few birds overwinter, mainly in the south.

### 149. Common Greenshank *Tringa nebularia*

✓ An uncommon passage migrant and winter visitor. It usually occurs near water bodies, mostly in coastal wetlands and sometimes inland. It can be seen mainly from August to April, but there are a few sightings outside this period.

### 150. Greater Yellowlegs *Tringa melanoleuca*

A very rare vagrant from the Nearctic, with only five records, all referring to singletons. Birds were seen at several coastal wetlands.

### 151. Cream-coloured Courser *Cursorius cursor*

A rare vagrant from North Africa, which has been recorded on ten occasions at different locations in the southern part of the country. All records were made between March and August, nearly half of them in the Algarve.

### 152. Collared Pratincole *Glareola pratincola*

✓ An uncommon summer visitor, which breeds locally in southern Portugal; there are several colonies in the Ribatejo, Alentejo and Algarve provinces. Sometimes turns up on passage further north, close to the coast. Arrives in late March and leaves in August.

### 153. Black-legged Kittiwake *Rissa tridactyla*

✓ An uncommon winter visitor, which is probably numerous away from the coast, although only rarely seen close to land. It occurs largely from October to March, with a few records at other times of the year. In 2009 there was a large 'invasion' of Black-legged Kittiwakes in Portugal and in that year there were many sightings in estuarine areas and even inland. Bred on Berlengas islands in 1981.

### 154. Ivory Gull *Pagophila eburnea*

A very rare vagrant from the Arctic regions which has been observed on a single occasion: an adult was present for a few days at Nazaré in November 2014.

### 155. Sabine's Gull *Xema sabini*

A passage migrant that is rare near the coast, but one that is probably frequent offshore, as there are several records from territorial waters and from the EEZ. All records were made between May and November.

### 156. Slender-billed Gull *Chroicocephalus genei*

Formerly considered a rarity, this gull is now regularly recorded in the eastern Algarve – there are many sightings from this region, in some cases involving tens of birds. Elsewhere the species is very rare and only a few sporadic records are known from other coastal wetlands.

### 157. Bonaparte's Gull *Chroicocephalus philadelphia*

There are 25 records of this Nearctic gull, most of them in the first quarter and all involving single birds. About half of the records come from the Estoril coast, near Lisbon, where a bird, probably the same returning individual, was regularly seen throughout almost the entire decade of 1990. The other records were made at various locations along the Portuguese coast.

### 158. Black-headed Gull *Chroicocephalus ridibundus*

A common winter visitor and passage migrant, which occurs mainly from July to March, although a few birds stay around during the breeding season. It can be seen throughout the country, but it is rare in the highlands and is generally more numerous near the coast than in the inland areas. Has bred at the Sado and Mondego estuaries and also in the eastern Alentejo.

## 159. Little Gull *Hydrocoloeus minutus*

A rare passage migrant and winter visitor, which can be found along the coast, both at coastal wetlands and on the open sea. Its main period of occurrence ranges from November to April, although there are some records on other months. Its numbers seem to vary a great deal between years; during the 2008-09 winter, Little Gulls were seen in unusually high numbers.

## 160. Laughing Gull *Leucophaeus atricilla*

A very rare vagrant, which has been recorded eight times at several coastal locations, from Douro Litoral south to the Algarve. Three records were made during autumn 2005 when there was an unprecedented influx of this Nearctic species into the Western Palearctic.

## 161. Franklin's Gull *Leucophaeus pipixcan*

Twelve records, all between 2003 and 2019. Half of them were made in the Lisbon region and the remaining ones at other coastal locations. All records refer to single birds.

## 162. Audouin's Gull *Ichthyaetus audouinii*

This gull is mainly recorded in the Algarve, where it is common and occurs regularly on migration and where a few overwinter. At the beginning of the 21st century, this species started to breed in the eastern Algarve, namely at Ria Formosa and Castro Marim. Its breeding population currently comprises about 1000 pairs. Outside the Algarve it is scarce, but the number of records has been increasing in recent years.

### 163. Mediterranean Gull *Ichthyaetus melanocephalus*

A common passage migrant and winter visitor, which can be found along the entire coastline. It is more frequent in the southern half of the country. The concentration of birds present at any given time fluctuates markedly, but numbers seem to be higher during periods of bad weather. This gull can be seen throughout the year, however, it is quite rare in spring.

### 164. Mew Gull *Larus canus*

A scarce winter visitor which is recorded annually but almost always in small numbers. It is more frequent along the coasts of northern and central Portugal and is quite rare in the south and in inland areas. Mainly seen from November to March, with occasional records in other months.

### 165. Ring-billed Gull *Larus delawarensis*

A rare winter visitor which has been recorded from September to May, with most records falling during the winter months. Almost all sightings involved single birds or small flocks and were made at beaches or coastal wetlands. Very rarely recorded inland.

### 166. Great Black-backed Gull *Larus marinus*

A scarce winter visitor, which is recorded annually along the coast, mostly in the northern and central regions and almost always in very small numbers. Most sightings are from the period ranging from September to March, but there are occasional records outside this period. From 2004 to 2009, one individual bred near Sintra, forming a mixed pair with a Yellow-legged Gull.

## 167. Kelp Gull *Larus dominicanus*

No records up to 2012, but the species has been recorded eight times since then, at several coastal locations, however, some sightings refer to the same returning individual. All records were made between late April and late August.

## 168. Glaucous Gull *Larus hyperboreus*

A rare winter visitor which is recorded almost every year in very small numbers. All records are from coastal areas and most took place from November to March, with a marked peak in January. There are isolated records from other times of the year. During the first three months of 2009, the number of records was well above average and the same happened at the beginning of 2014.

## 169. Iceland Gull *Larus glaucoides*

A rare winter visitor, which has been recorded about 80 times, always near the coast. Most records occurred between November and March and refer to single birds. During the first quarter of 2009 there was an influx and the number of sightings was unusually high, including two birds of the Nearctic subspecies *L. g. kumlieni*. In February 2014 there was another influx of birds of the race *kumlieni*, with at least five adults present.

## 170. European Herring Gull *Larus argentatus*

A rare winter visitor, seen mainly at beach locations or coastal wetlands. Most sightings refer to isolated birds or groups of two. Its period of occurrence ranges from September to March.

## 171. American Herring Gull *Larus smithsonianus*

A rare vagrant that has been recorded on 13 occasions, of which five in the north, six in the Estremadura and two in the Algarve. One record involved three different birds, the remaining ones refer to singletons. There is also a case of a bird that returned to the same location in successive years.

## 172. Caspian Gull *Larus cachinnans*

A rare vagrant which has been recorded 25 times. All known records took place between October and April, and most were made at coastal locations, but there is one record in the inner Alentejo. From 2013 onwards, the species has been reported every year.

## 173. Yellow-legged Gull *Larus michahellis*

C An abundant resident which can be found along the entire coast and, locally, in inland areas. Breeds on islands, islets, rocky coast and at certain coastal wetlands. In recent years it also started to nest in various coastal towns and at the Alto Rabagão reservoir, near Montalegre. The Berlengas islands, its main breeding site, hold several thousands of pairs, but the breeding population at this location is declining.

## 174. Lesser Black-backed Gull *Larus fuscus*

C An abundant passage migrant and winter visitor, which is seen mainly from July to March. It is more numerous along the coast, but can also be found inland, especially in the south. A few birds, mostly immature, remain in the country throughout the spring. Breeding seems to occur regularly in the Berlengas islands, albeit in very small numbers, and it has been occasionally reported from other locations.

## 175. Gull-billed Tern *Gelochelidon nilotica*

U An uncommon summer migrant, which occurs mainly in the eastern Alentejo, where it breeds near large or medium-sized reservoirs. May turn up at other places in central and southern Portugal during migration times. Usually occurs in the country from March to September. Occasionally recorded in winter.

## 176. Caspian Tern *Hydroprogne caspia*

A scarce passage migrant and winter visitor, that occurs in small numbers in coastal wetlands in southern Portugal. It is more frequent in the Algarve than elsewhere, but there are also several records at the Tejo and Sado estuaries and a few inland. Mostly recorded from October to April, with isolated records during other months.

## 177. Royal Tern *Thalasseus maximus*

Only four records, all in the Algarve: the first at Ria de Alvor, Portimão, in October 1991; the second at the same place in April 1996; and the last two in the Castro Marim reserve in August 2006 and August 2019, respectively.

## 178. Lesser Crested Tern *Thalasseus bengalensis*

Eleven recent records, all at coastal locations between May and October. During the last decade, it has been recorded almost every year. One of the birds was seen near Porto, four in the Lisbon region and the other six in the Algarve.

## 179. Sandwich Tern *Thalasseus sandvicensis*

C A common passage migrant and uncommon winter visitor. It can be seen along the coast and may be locally abundant on migration. It is rare inland, but may occasionally fly along the major rivers up to a few tens of kilometres from the river mouth.

## 180. Elegant Tern *Thalasseus elegans*

One at Dafundo Beach, Oeiras, in August 2011.

## 181. Little Tern *Sternula albifrons*

∪ An uncommon summer visitor and passage migrant. Breeds at the main coastal wetlands in central and southern Portugal, locally also at some reservoirs in the eastern Alentejo. It is more common in the eastern Algarve than elsewhere. Also seen on migration along the coast. Its main period of occurrence ranges from April to September, but occasionally it is recorded in winter, especially in the Algarve.

## 182. Bridled Tern *Onychoprion anaethetus*

A single record is known: a bird was found in Lisbon in December 2019. This bird was very weak and died on the same day it was found.

## 183. Sooty Tern *Onychoprion fuscatus*

A very rare vagrant recorded only twice: one at Barra beach, Aveiro, in August 1988 and another one at Peniche in April 2017.

## 184. Roseate Tern *Sterna dougallii*

A rare passage migrant, which has been recorded about 25 times. All records have been made along the coasts of central or southern Portugal and refer to single birds or small groups of up to three. Cape Carvoeiro and Cape Raso are the two places with most records. Sightings were made both during the pre-nuptial migration, from late April to early June, and during the post-nuptial one, between August and October. There are very few records outside this period.

## 185. Common Tern *Sterna hirundo*

( A common passage migrant, which is recorded mostly near the coast and, occasionally, inland. The pre-nuptial passage occurs mostly in April and May, while the post-nuptial one ranges from August to October. However, this tern is sometimes seen in other months, even in midwinter. Breeding has been irregularly recorded in the Tagus and Sado estuaries.

## 186. Arctic Tern *Sterna paradisaea*

An uncommon passage migrant which occurs regularly during migration periods along the Portuguese coast, especially on the open sea. The pre-nuptial passage is from March to May, whereas post-nuptial passage takes place from August to October. There are isolated records outside this period.

## 187. Forster's Tern *Sterna forsteri*

A very rare vagrant, recorded on three occasions: one at Castro Marim, in December 1993; another one at Fuseta, Olhão, in February 2003; and the last one at Peniche, from November 2010 until January 2011.

## 188. Whiskered Tern *Chlidonias hybrida*

An uncommon summer visitor and passage migrant, which is highly irregular – it can be frequent in certain years and be almost absent in others. Has bred in the Beira Litoral, Ribatejo and Alentejo provinces, mostly in marshes or reservoirs. When on migration, it can also turn up at coastal wetlands. Usually appears between April and September.

## 189. White-winged Tern *Chlidonias leucopterus*

A rare passage migrant which has been recorded about 60 times. Sightings refer to single birds or groups of two, but on one occasion five birds were seen together. Almost all records were made during the period ranging from April to October at coastal locations – the areas with more observations are the Tagus estuary and the Algarve south coast.

## 190. Black Tern *Chlidonias niger*

✓ An uncommon passage migrant that turns up in highly variable numbers in different years. It occurs at coastal wetlands and sometimes inland. During post-nuptial migration, it can also be found on the open sea. Spring passage usually takes place in April and May, autumn passage extends from August to October. Has bred in the Algarve.

## 191. South Polar Skua *Stercorarius maccormicki*

One seen and photographed off Guincho Beach, Cascais, in November 2007.

## 192. Great Skua *Stercorarius skua*

∪ An uncommon winter visitor which is regular at sea off the Portuguese coast. It is often recorded from land, especially under bad weather. It occurs mainly from October to March, with occasional sightings at other times of the year. Its period of occurrence largely coincides with that of the Northern Gannet, which is its main victim of cleptoparasitism.

## 193. Pomarine Jaeger *Stercorarius pomarinus*

∪ An uncommon passage migrant, which is regular offshore; not infrequently, it is seen by land-based observers, usually in small numbers, but can be abundant when severe serial storms occur at sea. The spring passage takes place in March and April, while the autumn passage happens from August to November. Occasionally seen in winter.

## 194. Parasitic Jaeger *Stercorarius parasiticus*

C A non-breeding visitor along Portuguese coasts, which is common on migration. Spring passage happens in April and May, whereas autumn passage takes place from August to October. This skua can also be found in small numbers during the winter months, especially in the south.

## 195. Long-tailed Jaeger *Stercorarius longicaudus*

A scarce passage migrant, which is only occasionally seen from land but which is regular offshore. Most records were made between August and October, but there are also a few spring records. Cape Raso and Cape Carvoeiro are the two places where this skua has been recorded more frequently.

## 196. Little Auk *Alle alle*

About ten records are known, from different points along the coast between October and February. Most records refer to birds found dead on beaches.

## 197. Common Murre *Uria aalge*

Nowadays a rare winter visitor. The Berlengas archipelago used to hold the only breeding population, which had been declining for many decades. At present, the species no longer breeds there, but isolated birds are seen in the area from time to time.

## 198. Razorbill *Alca torda*

C A common winter visitor to Portuguese seas, which can regularly be seen from land, mainly from October to March. Sometimes it turns up in harbours or coastal wetlands. Dead birds are frequently found on beaches, often because of trapping in fishing nets or severe storms.

## 199. Atlantic Puffin *Fratercula arctica*

𝒰 An uncommon passage migrant and winter visitor, which is regular offshore but is only occasionally seen from land. However, there are many records of dead bodies found on beaches, usually after severe weather. Its main period of occurrence extends from October to March, with a few scattered records at other times of the year.

## 200. Red-billed Tropicbird *Phaethon aethereus*

A very rare visitor from the Afrotropics. Only one record is known along the Portuguese coast: a bird was seen at Cape Carvoeiro in September 2015. There is also a record from the EEZ, about 100 nautical miles west of Cape Sardão, in August 1988.

## 201. Red-throated Loon *Gavia stellata*

A rare winter visitor, which turns up every year in very small numbers. About 70 records are known, usually involving single birds or small parties of up to four birds, seen on the open sea by land-based observers or in coastal wetlands.

## 202. Black-throated Loon *Gavia arctica*

A very rare vagrant, with only six records in recent years. All records were made between October and March, at coastal wetlands. Singles were seen on all but one occasion when two birds were involved. There is also an old record from the 19th century referring to a bird seen in the Ria de Aveiro.

## 203. Common Loon *Gavia immer*

A rare winter visitor, which is seen every year in small numbers. Most records come from along the coastline, especially in the Sado estuary where the species is regular.

Dates range from November to early May, with a marked peak in December.

## 204. Wilson's Storm Petrel *Oceanites oceanicus*

C A common passage migrant in Portuguese waters, although it occurs mainly offshore and is rarely seen from land. Record dates span from May to October, with a peak during summer months.

## 205. White-faced Storm Petrel *Pelagodroma marina*

A rare vagrant or possibly a regular passage migrant from Macaronesian waters. There are ten records in the EEZ, nearly all in August and all involving one or two birds. There are also two records in the Sagres area.

## 206. Wandering Albatross *Diomedea exulans*

One record: a bird seen about 40 miles southwest of Cape St. Vincent, in October 1963.

## 207. Black-browed Albatross *Thalassarche melanophris*

One near the Berlengas islands in February 1983.

## 208. European Storm Petrel *Hydrobates pelagicus*

A regular passage migrant, rarely seen from land but which is common offshore. Its occurrence in Portuguese waters ranges, at least, from May to October.

## 209. Band-rumped Storm Petrel *Oceanodroma castro*

Breeds in the Farilhões, a small group of islets which are part of the Berlengas archipelago, and sometimes it is seen in the surrounding areas. Very rarely observed elsewhere.

## 210. Swinhoe's Storm Petrel *Oceanodroma monorhis*

Two records are known, both referring to birds trapped and ringed at Ponta da Almádena, Lagos during European Storm Petrel ringing sessions. The first was in June 1998 and the other one in June 2017.

## 211. Leach's Storm Petrel *Oceanodroma leucorhoa*

An uncommon passage migrant and winter visitor, seen mainly from October to February. Its appearance near the coast is usually related to the occurrence of storms, when this petrel is often seen by land-based observers flying over the sea or even at coastal wetlands. Additionally, on these occasions, dead birds are sometimes found on beaches or even inland.

## 212. Northern Fulmar *Fulmarus glacialis*

A rare vagrant which has been recorded on several occasions along the Portuguese coast, mostly as beached corpses, during winter months. There are also a few records of birds seen on passage from land and one farther offshore.

## 213. Fea's Petrel *Pterodroma deserta*

Only two records are known of this species which breeds in the Macaronesian islands: a bird in the EEZ off Viana do Castelo in August 2008 and another one near Cape Carvoeiro in September 2015.

## 214. Scopoli's Shearwater *Calonectris diomedea*

This shearwater might be regular along the Portuguese south coast, however, the current status of this species, which was recently separated from Cory's Shearwater, remains unclear.

## 215. Cory's Shearwater *Calonectris borealis*

⌄ The Berlengas archipelago, where a few hundred pairs breed, holds the only colony near mainland Portugal, but the species can be seen along the entire coast, sometimes in large numbers. It is usually present from late February to November, being rare during winter months.

## 216. Sooty Shearwater *Ardenna grisea*

∨ An uncommon passage migrant, which occurs mostly from August to October. Although it is more abundant offshore, it is regularly seen from land, usually in small numbers, but under certain weather conditions, the count may reach several tens per hour.

## 217. Great Shearwater *Ardenna gravis*

∨ An uncommon passage migrant close to the coast which is, however, quite numerous offshore. It turns up in Portuguese waters during late summer and early autumn, mainly from mid-August to October. Sometimes it is seen from land.

## 218. Manx Shearwater *Puffinus puffinus*

⌄ An uncommon passage migrant, which has been recorded at different times of the year. Its passage seems to be stronger during late summer and early autumn.

## 219. Balearic Shearwater *Puffinus mauretanicus*

⌄ A non-breeding visitor which can be found year round over Portuguese waters, with two peaks of abundance: the first in early summer and the second in early autumn. Can regularly be seen from land, often in considerable numbers.

### 220. Barolo Shearwater *Puffinus baroli*

A scarce but probably regular passage migrant, originating from the Macaronesian islands. Rather rare in coastal waters, from where less than ten records are known, most of them in September and October – however, there are about twenty records in July and August in the southern part of the EEZ, where the species is probably regular.

### 221. Bulwer's Petrel *Bulweria bulwerii*

Breeds in the Macaronesian islands and is regular in the EEZ waters, especially during summer and autumn, however, it prefers areas beyond the continental platform and seldom turns up at coastal waters.

### 222. Black Stork *Ciconia nigra*

A rare summer visitor, which has a breeding population of around 100 pairs. It occurs mostly in the eastern half of the country, from Trás-os-Montes to the Baixo Alentejo. Birds on passage can also be found near the coast, particularly in the Algarve. The species usually arrives in March and departs in September or October, however, a few birds remain in the country throughout the winter, mainly in the south – this pattern has been increasing during the last decade.

### 223. White Stork *Ciconia ciconia*

A partial migrant which occurs throughout the country, although it is rare in the northwest and over much of the centre-west. It is very numerous in the Ribatejo and Alentejo provinces and also in the lower Mondego and Vouga valleys. A part of the population, which comprises some adults and almost all young birds, moves to Africa during late summer, but many adult birds remain in Portugal throughout the year. Additionally, there is a wintering population formed by birds from central Europe.

## 224. Northern Gannet *Morus bassanus*

Ɛ A common passage migrant and winter visitor. Although it can be seen along the Portuguese coast throughout the year, it is more numerous from October to April. During summer months, most sightings refer to immature birds.

## 225. Red-footed Booby *Sula sula*

A juvenile was seen at Cape Sardão, Odemira, in June 2019.

## 226. Brown Booby *Sula leucogaster*

Only ten records are known. Six of them were made along the coasts of Estremadura and the other four in the Algarve. All records refer to single birds and dates span from March to October, with a peak in July.

## 227. European Shag *Phalacrocorax aristotelis*

∨ An uncommon resident, which breeds in the Berlengas archipelago and in some sectors of rocky coast, namely in Estremadura, Alentejo and Algarve. Only rarely seen away from these areas. There are a few records along the coast of northern Portugal, which may refer to birds wandering from Galicia, in north-western Spain, where it also breeds.

## 228. Great Cormorant *Phalacrocorax carbo*

C A common winter visitor, which is present mainly from September to March, although small numbers can be seen during spring and summer months. It occurs throughout the country but is more numerous near the coast than inland. Breeding has been recorded in recent years, both at the Alqueva reservoir and at the Boquilobo marsh; its breeding population comprises over 200 breeding pairs.

### 229. Glossy Ibis *Plegadis falcinellus*

*C* A common winter visitor with a very patchy distribution. It can be found in Portugal throughout the year, but it is more numerous during autumn and winter months, particularly at coastal wetlands, and it can be locally abundant in the Tagus and Sado estuaries and at certain places in the Algarve. Elsewhere it is generally scarce. In recent years it has bred along the Tagus basin, namely in the Boquilobo marsh, at Escaroupim (Salvaterra de Magos) and at the Tagus estuary; breeding has also been confirmed in the Sado valley and at the Taipal marsh.

### 230. Eurasian Spoonbill *Platalea leucorodia*

A scarce and localized breeding species, of which there are about twenty colonies, almost all of them located south of the River Tagus. Its breeding population seems to be expanding and new colonies have been found in recent years. It is also an uncommon passage migrant and winter visitor, which occurs regularly in most coastal wetlands and occasionally in inland waters. Sometimes flocks of up to a few hundred birds are recorded, especially in the Algarve.

### 231. Eurasian Bittern *Botaurus stellaris*

A rare winter visitor which turns up almost every year, albeit in very small numbers. Most sightings took place between November and March, but there are a few records from other months. The last breeding confirmation took place in 1987 at the Açude da Murta, Alcácer do Sal. There are a few more isolated records during the breeding season, and the species may breed sporadically at other coastal wetlands.

### 232. Little Bittern *Ixobrychus minutus*

A scarce breeding visitor, which favours coastal wetlands, but it can also be locally found inland in the southern half of the country. Rare elsewhere. It occurs largely from April to September. In the Algarve, there are several records during the winter months and a small wintering population exists there.

## 233. Black-crowned Night Heron *Nycticorax nycticorax*

A scarce summer visitor, which breeds colonially, mainly in the lower Tagus, Sado and Mondego basins, locally also in the inner Alentejo. The large colonies that existed in the Guadiana valley up to the 1990s have been abandoned. In recent years, this species has been regularly recorded in winter.

## 234. Green Heron *Butorides virescens*

A very rare vagrant. Only two records are known, both in November 2018: one bird was found at Quinta do Lago, Loulé, and it stayed until April 2019; the other one was at Aroeira, Almada.

## 235. Squacco Heron *Ardeola ralloides*

A rare passage migrant and winter visitor, which is seen every year in Portugal, but always in very small numbers. The species has been recorded in every month of the year, mostly in coastal wetland areas. Has bred several times at the Boquilobo marsh and, occasionally, at other locations in the Ribatejo and Alentejo provinces.

## 236. Western Cattle Egret *Bubulcus ibis*

A common resident. Breeds colonially, often forming mixed colonies with other herons. Its colonies lie mainly south of the River Tagus, with only a few ones to the north of this river. During autumn and winter, this egret often turns up in northern and central Portugal, but usually in small numbers.

### 237. Grey Heron *Ardea cinerea*

*U*  Uncommon as a breeding species, but numerous as a winter visitor. Can be found throughout the country, in any kind of wetland. It is particularly numerous in coastal wetlands. Breeds isolated or in colonies, mostly to the south of the River Tagus.

### 238. Purple Heron *Ardea purpurea*

*U*  An uncommon summer visitor, which breeds mainly in coastal wetlands. The Ria de Aveiro and the Tagus estuary are the two strongholds of this species. Quite rare inland. Usually arrives in March and departs in September, with very few records in other months.

### 239. Great Egret *Ardea alba*

A scarce winter visitor, which can be seen mainly from October to March, although there are a few records outside this period. Up to the 1990s, this species was very rare in Portugal, but in recent years it has gradually become more frequent and nowadays it is regular in certain areas, especially in the south and in the western part of central Portugal. Its wintering population comprises several hundred birds. The first breeding confirmation came in 2016 from the Boquilobo marsh.

### 240. Little Egret *Egretta garzetta*

*C*  A common resident, found in wetland areas throughout the country, mostly near the coast but also inland. Breeds in colonies, often in association with the Western Cattle Egret. Almost all colonies lie south of the River Tagus.

### 241. Western Reef Heron *Egretta gularis*

A rare vagrant, of which only six records are known, all referring to single individuals. Sightings were made between February and September at several locations in the central and southern parts of the country. Additionally, there are a few records of birds that might be hybrids *E. gularis* x *E. garzetta*.

## 242. Western Osprey *Pandion haliaetus*

An uncommon passage migrant and winter visitor. Usually seen close to large water bodies, mainly estuaries, large rivers, coastal lagoons and reservoirs, therefore it is more frequently seen near the coast. The wintering population comprises nearly 200 birds. Bred at several locations along the southwest coast, up to the end of the 20th century, and bred again in this area in 2015. In 2011 a reintroduction project started at the Alqueva reservoir, aiming at establishing a breeding population; as part of this project, several young birds were released there in that same year and in the following ones, and breeding was recorded in that area from 2015 to 2019.

## 243. Black-winged Kite *Elanus caeruleus*

An uncommon resident which occurs mainly in the southern half of the country and also in the Beira Interior. It is rare to the north of the River Douro. It is more numerous in the eastern Alentejo than elsewhere. However, it seems to be expanding and there are recent breeding records from the Algarve, the southwest coast and in certain areas of coastal provinces in the centre. During autumn and winter, it occurs regularly in small numbers at several places of Beira Litoral and at other coastal locations where it does not breed.

## 244. Bearded Vulture *Gypaetus barbatus*

Two birds (an adult and a juvenile) were shot in the River Guadiana by the late King Carlos I in June 1888. These birds are kept in the University Museum of Coimbra. More recently, in May and June 2011, two birds that had been released in southern Spain as part of a reintroduction project that is being undertaken, briefly flew over Portuguese territory, close to the Spanish border in Beira and Trás-os-Montes. In the following years, there were a few more records of Spanish birds that visited Portuguese territory.

### 245. Egyptian Vulture *Neophron percnopterus*

An uncommon summer visitor, which breeds mainly along the international sectors of the Douro and Tagus rivers, and also along some of their tributaries. Very rare as a breeding bird south of the River Tagus. Its population is currently estimated at 120 pairs. It occurs mainly from late February to October, but there are scattered records in other months. Can be seen on migration in other parts of the country, particularly at Cape St. Vincent, where it is regular during post-nuptial passage.

### 246. European Honey Buzzard *Pernis apivorus*

An uncommon summer migrant, which breeds sparsely throughout the country, usually at low density. As a breeding bird, it is more frequent in the northern part and is quite rare to the south of the River Tagus. Its main period of occurrence spans from April to October. Regularly seen during the post-nuptial passage, especially in September, at Cape St. Vincent and sometimes elsewhere along the coast.

### 247. White-backed Vulture *Gyps africanus*

A very rare vagrant from the Afrotropics, seen only on two occasions: one bird was at Cape St. Vincent in October 2006 and another one was seen near Mourão in August 2014.

## 248. Rüppell's Vulture *Gyps rueppellii*

About 60 records are known, most of them referring to single birds, but there are a few records involving two, three or even five individuals seen together. Sightings come from two distinct areas: on one hand, the upper Tagus valley and the northern Alentejo, where the species has been seen throughout the year and breeding was proved in 1999, and also the Portas de Ródão, near Vila Velha de Ródão, where breeding may have happened (at the latter site, one individual was resident for at least five years and was seen building a nest, which it occupied), and on the other hand, there is the southern region formed by Baixo Alentejo and Algarve, where the species turns up mainly on autumn migration. There are also a few records in the Beira Alta province and in the northeastern province of Trás-os-Montes.

## 249. Griffon Vulture *Gyps fulvus*

An uncommon resident, which occurs mainly over eastern Portugal. Breeds inland chiefly to the north of the River Tagus, and it can be locally common, whereas in the northern Alentejo it breeds in small numbers only. It can also be seen throughout the year in several places where it does not breed, especially in the eastern Alentejo and Beira provinces. Its population comprises about 1000 breeding pairs. In autumn, these vultures turn up regularly far away from breeding areas, notably in the western Algarve, where flocks of several hundred or even over one thousand birds have been reported on several occasions.

## 250. Cinereous Vulture *Aegypius monachus*

A rare resident which can be found throughout the year. It is regular along the Spanish border in the Beira and Alentejo regions (where at least three hundred different individuals certainly occur), but it is much scarcer as one moves westwards and only occasionally is it seen near the coast.

After a prolonged absence of several decades as a breeding bird, and after a few failed nesting attempts, it started breeding in 2010 and currently nests at several inland locations. The national breeding population is estimated at about 30 pairs.

## 251. Short-toed Snake Eagle *Circaetus gallicus*

An uncommon summer migrant, which occurs throughout the country, although it is very scarce in the western provinces that lie north of the River Tagus. It can be seen mainly from March to September, however, there are over one hundred winter records, most of them in the Algarve.

## 252. Lesser Spotted Eagle *Clanga pomarina*

There are about 20 records of singletons in the Vila do Bispo area, all during the post-nuptial migration, between late September and mid-November. In autumn 2017 the number of records was above average – this suggests that a small influx may have taken place.

## 253. Greater Spotted Eagle *Clanga clanga*

About ten records are known from the Tagus estuary and one from the Sado estuary. All these records were made between October and March in the period ranging from 1998 to 2004 and they may refer to the same returning individual.

## 254. Booted Eagle *Hieraaetus pennatus*

An uncommon but widespread summer visitor which breeds over most of the country, although it is rare in the northwest and in the Algarve. During migration, it can often be found in places where it does not breed, particularly at Cape St. Vincent, where several hundred birds pass every autumn. A few individuals remain throughout the winter season, mainly in the south and in some coastal wetlands in central Portugal.

## 255. Spanish Imperial Eagle *Aquila adalberti*

A rare resident, which was absent for several decades as a breeding species but which has recently recolonised the country. It breeds in small numbers in the east, namely in the Beira Baixa and also in the Alentejo. The population comprises about 20 breeding pairs. Juvenile and immature birds are regularly seen in the Alentejo and sometimes elsewhere; there are several autumn records in coastal areas.

## 256. Golden Eagle *Aquila chrysaetos*

A rare resident which occurs mainly inland, but its distribution is very discontinuous. It is more frequent in the north-eastern province of Trás-os-Montes, but small numbers breed in the Beira Baixa and in certain areas of the eastern Alentejo as well. Its breeding population is probably over 90 pairs. Young birds sometimes wander far away from breeding areas.

## 257. Bonelli's Eagle *Aquila fasciata*

An uncommon resident, which is patchily distributed. It occurs mainly in eastern Portugal, although it can also be found locally in western areas in the southern half of the country. The provinces of Algarve, Baixo Alentejo and Trás-os-Montes are those where this eagle is more common. Its population has been recovering in the last few decades and currently exceeds 130 breeding pairs.

## 258. Eurasian Sparrowhawk *Accipiter nisus*

An uncommon resident, passage migrant and winter visitor. Breeds mainly to the north of the River Tagus, further south it is scarce in spring but turns up regularly in small numbers during autumn and winter.

## 259. Northern Goshawk *Accipiter gentilis*

An uncommon resident and winter visitor, which occurs mainly in the north-western part of the country and is rare elsewhere. Hard to detect, as it lives mostly in dense woodland. During winter, numbers increase slightly due to the presence of migrants and at this time of year the species is more frequently recorded in areas where it does not breed.

## 260. Western Marsh Harrier *Circus aeruginosus*

An uncommon resident and winter visitor, it occurs mainly in coastal wetlands, being rather scarce inland. The most important sites for this harrier are the Ria de Aveiro and the Tagus and Sado estuaries – in all these areas, the species can be considered as locally common. In the smaller wetlands, its presence is somewhat irregular. Its national population seems to be increasing and expanding. In recent years, this harrier was found breeding in cereal fields or small reservoirs at several locations in the Alentejo.

## 261. Hen Harrier *Circus cyaneus*

A rare breeder and an uncommon winter visitor. As a breeding bird, it can be found almost exclusively in the highlands lying north of the River Douro and, occasionally, in the Beira Interior. Its breeding population probably does not exceed 30 pairs. In autumn and winter, it can also be seen regularly in central and southern Portugal, usually in small numbers.

## 262. Northern Harrier *Circus hudsonius*

A male was seen near Murtosa in February and March 2018.

### 263. Pallid Harrier *Circus macrourus*

Up to 2010, this species had never been recorded in Portugal, however, since 2011 this harrier has been seen every year in the southern half of the country. About 50 records are known, most of them south of the River Tagus. Some of these birds overwintered. In the case of the Tagus estuary, up to three different individuals have been recorded there in the same winter.

### 264. Montagu's Harrier *Circus pygargus*

An uncommon summer migrant, which breeds mainly in the eastern half of the country; to the north of the River Tagus it favours highlands, whereas in the south it occurs mainly in the open plains, where it can be locally common, however recent data suggests that its population is declining. It is usually present from March to September.

### 265. Red Kite *Milvus milvus*

A rare breeder which occurs in small numbers along the Spanish border, mainly in the northeast and locally in the Alto Alentejo. Its breeding population has been declining sharply and is probably of less than 50 pairs. It is also an uncommon winter visitor, which appears between October and March, mainly in the eastern Alentejo, where it is locally common, and in Beira Interior, with occasional sightings elsewhere. Roosts with hundreds of birds exist in the Castro Verde area.

### 266. Black Kite *Milvus migrans*

A common summer visitor, which breeds throughout the country. It is more abundant in the Mondego basin and over the eastern Alentejo. The first birds are usually seen in late February or early March, while most departures take place in August. However, there are a few records outside this period, even in midwinter, mostly near sanitary landfills.

Often seen on passage at places where it does not breed, particularly along the coast.

### 267. White-tailed Eagle *Haliaeetus albicilla*

Two old records are known: one of a bird shot in 1902 by King Carlos I at Cascais, and the other one of a bird shot in Serra da Estrela in the 1960s or 1970s. No recent records.

### 268. Long-legged Buzzard *Buteo rufinus*

Several records, not accepted by the PRC but attributed to this species, have been published, all from southern Portugal, namely from the Alentejo and Algarve provinces.

### 269. Common Buzzard *Buteo buteo*

C  A common resident which can be found throughout the country.

### 270. Barn Owl *Tyto alba*

C  A common and widespread resident. From late summer onwards, considerable numbers occur in certain areas, like the plains of the lower Tagus valley, where it sometimes turns up in very high densities.

### 271. Eurasian Scops Owl *Otus scops*

✓  This is an uncommon summer visitor to Portugal, which occurs mostly between March and October. It has a widespread distribution and is clearly more frequent in the north-eastern provinces of Trás-os-Montes and Beira Interior, where it can be locally common. It is regularly recorded on passage away from breeding areas, particularly along the coast of the Algarve. A few wintering records are known from southern areas.

## 272. Eurasian Eagle-Owl *Bubo bubo*

An uncommon resident which occurs mostly in remote inland areas, but locally also closer to the coast. It seems to be more numerous along the valleys of the Guadiana and the upper Tagus rivers, as well as along those of their tributaries. Its population probably exceeds 500 pairs.

## 273. Tawny Owl *Strix aluco*

A common resident which occurs throughout the country. It seems to be more frequent in the southern half.

## 274. Little Owl *Athene noctua*

A common and widespread resident that is more numerous in the south, particularly in the eastern Alentejo and in the Algarve.

## 275. Long-eared Owl *Asio otus*

A scarce resident. Its distribution area is poorly known, due to its shy habits. Probably occurs over most of the country, usually at low density. Outside the breeding season, it is sometimes found close to the coast, in places where breeding is not known. Winter roosts are known in several towns.

## 276. Short-eared Owl *Asio flammeus*

A rare winter visitor, which arrives in late September and stays until March or April. It seems to be more frequent near the coast, especially around wetlands. There are very few records inland, although the species is known to occur at times in cereal fields in the eastern part of the Alentejo.

### 277. Marsh Owl *Asio capensis*

Two birds were shot in the Tagus estuary in the late 19th century. This is the only record.

### 278. Eurasian Hoopoe *Upupa epops*

C A partial migrant which can be seen throughout the country and is generally a common bird. Its status varies according to the regions: in the north and much of the centre it is mainly a summer visitor, arriving in March, but to the south of the River Tagus and in some areas further north it can be seen year-round.

### 279. European Roller *Coracias garrulus*

A scarce summer breeder, which occurs almost exclusively in the open plains of the eastern Alentejo and locally in Beira Baixa. Birds on passage often turn up elsewhere, namely near the coastline or in the northern highlands. It is usually found between April and mid-September. Its breeding population probably comprises between 100 and 150 pairs; most of these occur in the Castro Verde area.

### 280. Common Kingfisher *Alcedo atthis*

A resident and dispersive species which occurs throughout the country. Generally uncommon and mostly seen isolated or in pairs. It can be considered frequent in the largest wetlands, especially outside the breeding season. It is rare in the highlands.

### 281. Blue-cheeked Bee-eater *Merops persicus*

A very rare vagrant from North Africa, which has been recorded twice: one was at Piçarras, Castro Verde, in April 2014 and the other one was seen near Tavira in April 2016. On both occasions, birds were seen in association with European Bee-eaters.

## 282. European Bee-eater *Merops apiaster*

A common summer visitor, which occurs throughout the country as far north as Trás-os-Montes, although it is absent from the western half north of the River Tagus. It is more frequent in the eastern Alentejo and over most of Beira Baixa province. Usually arrives in late March and leaves in mid-September.

## 283. Eurasian Wryneck *Jynx torquilla*

An uncommon summer breeder and passage migrant, the Wryneck has a very patchy distribution covering several regions of the country. It is more numerous in the north-eastern province of Trás-os-Montes. It occurs mostly between April and October, but it is regularly recorded in small numbers during the winter months, especially in the south.

## 284. Lesser Spotted Woodpecker *Dryobates minor*

An uncommon resident with a wide but discontinuous range. It is more frequent in the southern half of Ribatejo province and in the basin of the River Sado than elsewhere; it is quite rare north of the River Douro and is virtually absent from the western provinces lying north of the River Tagus.

## 285. Great Spotted Woodpecker *Dendrocopos major*

A common and widespread resident, which is more frequent in the western half of the country.

## 286. Iberian Green Woodpecker *Picus sharpei*

This resident woodpecker can be found over most of the country, although it seems to be absent in certain parts of the Alentejo. It is generally uncommon but is more numerous in the northwest, where it can be locally common.

### 287. Lesser Kestrel *Falco naumanni*

An uncommon breeding visitor, which occurs almost only in the southeast, particularly in the Baixo Alentejo; can be found locally at other places south of the River Tagus. It is usually present between February and August. The Portuguese population underwent a strong recovery in the last 20 years, mainly because of conservation projects aimed at this species; it comprises about 500 breeding pairs.

### 288. Common Kestrel *Falco tinnunculus*

A common and widespread resident, which is however somewhat infrequent in the north-western provinces of Minho and Douro Litoral. It is particularly abundant in Estremadura.

### 289. Red-footed Falcon *Falco vespertinus*

In most years it is very rare and up to 2014 only about ten records were known, most of them in September. In May 2015 an unprecedented movement took place and there were records from many locations in central and southern Portugal, in some cases involving small flocks. The largest flock comprised 21 birds and was seen near Baleizão, Beja.

### 290. Eleonora's Falcon *Falco eleonorae*

An uncommon passage migrant, which has been recorded at various locations in the centre and south, mostly along the coast. Dates of observation range from April to November, with most records in August and September.

## 291. Merlin *Falco columbarius*

A very scarce winter visitor, which can be seen from October to March. Although there are records from all over the country, it seems to be more frequent in the southern half. Almost always seen isolated, mostly in open areas.

## 292. Eurasian Hobby *Falco subbuteo*

A widespread summer visitor, which occurs in low densities over most of the country. It is more frequent north of the River Tagus, particularly in Beira Litoral and Beira Alta; in the south, it is rare as a breeding bird, but can be regularly seen on passage. It is present mainly from April to October.

## 293. Lanner Falcon *Falco biarmicus*

This falcon has been recorded on several occasions in the Alentejo and Algarve provinces.

## 294. Saker Falcon *Falco cherrug*

A single record is known: a bird followed by satellite tracking briefly visited Portuguese territory in August 2009, namely in the areas of Ribacoa and Serra da Estrela. This bird had been tagged in Hungary.

## 295. Peregrine Falcon *Falco peregrinus*

An uncommon and localised resident and possibly also a winter visitor, which has a notably discontinuous distribution in Portugal. During the breeding season, it can usually be found around cliffs; to the north of Nazaré, it occurs mainly inland, whereas further south it favours coastal areas. Its breeding population has about 120 pairs. At other times of the year it turns up frequently away from breeding areas, namely on wetlands or in open country.

### 296. Rose-ringed Parakeet *Psittacula krameri*

An uncommon and localised resident. This parakeet is native to Asia and Africa but was introduced to Portugal, probably during the 1970s. A small wild population became established in Lisbon and in the surrounding areas, and birds can be seen regularly in many city parks. There are also small breeding populations in Porto and Caldas da Rainha. Elsewhere it is a rare bird, scattered records are known from several areas, namely in the coastal provinces of northern and central parts of the country, as well as in Ribatejo, in eastern Alentejo and in the Algarve.

### 297. Red-backed Shrike *Lanius collurio*

A scarce summer migrant, which breeds in the northern highlands, namely in the Alto Minho and Trás-os-Montes provinces, most notably at Terras de Barroso, where it is locally common. It is very rare south of the River Douro, even on migration, but has bred in central Portugal. It is present in the country from mid-May to early September.

### 298. Red-tailed Shrike *Lanius phoenicuroides*

A single record is known: a bird was seen in the Vila Franca de Xira plains in July 2018.

### 299. Lesser Grey Shrike *Lanius minor*

One at Sagres, Vila do Bispo, in September 2019.

### 300. Iberian Grey Shrike *Lanius meridionalis*

An uncommon but widespread resident, possibly also a winter visitor. As a breeding species, it occurs over most of the country and is more frequent in the eastern Alentejo. In the western half, north of Cape Carvoeiro it is scarce and is mainly a non-breeding visitor.

## 301. Woodchat Shrike *Lanius senator*

A common summer visitor which arrives in March and leaves in September. It occurs over most of the south and also in Beira Interior and in a large part of the northeast. It is generally more abundant in the areas lying close to the Spanish border, however, birds on passage can regularly be seen in coastal areas.

## 302. Red-eyed Vireo *Vireo olivaceus*

One was seen near Ovar, in October 2018. This is the only record.

## 303. Eurasian Golden Oriole *Oriolus oriolus*

An uncommon but widespread summer visitor which occurs over most of the country. Its abundance is highly variable and the species is generally scarce in the western half and more common inland. The areas of greatest abundance lie in the north-eastern province of Trás-os-Montes, in the Beira Interior and in the area of lower Guadiana. It occurs mainly between mid-April and mid-September.

## 304. Eurasian Jay *Garrulus glandarius*

A common and widespread resident. Its abundance varies between regions, the species being more frequent in the north.

## 305. Iberian Magpie *Cyanopica cooki*

This is a resident species which occurs mainly in the south and in the eastern part of the centre; it can also be locally found in the northeast, namely along the International Douro. It is more abundant in the areas of Beira Interior lying close to the Spanish border and in the extreme southeast, along the basin of the River Guadiana. It seems to be expanding, at least in the southwest and also in Beira Interior.

### 306. Eurasian Magpie *Pica pica*

A widespread resident. Its abundance varies markedly between regions. It is uncommon north of the River Tagus, except in the Beira Interior region, where it is locally common; in the south, it is common in the Alto Alentejo, however, it is very scarce over much of Baixo Alentejo. In the Algarve, it can be found mainly in coastal areas.

### 307. Spotted Nutcracker *Nucifraga caryocatactes*

Four records are known of this rare vagrant, all from before 1970. Two come from the Alentejo and one from Estarreja. As to the fourth record, its location remains unknown.

### 308. Red-billed Chough *Pyrrhocorax pyrrhocorax*

A rare resident, which concentrates at a few places, namely in the Serras of Gerês and Candeeiros, in the International Douro area and at Cape St. Vincent. In the case of Serra da Estrela, the Chough was formerly regular, but this is no longer the case and it is only occasionally seen there. Very rarely seen in other parts of the country.

### 309. Western Jackdaw *Coloeus monedula*

A scarce resident with a highly discontinuous distribution; it occurs mainly in the eastern half of the country and also in coastal locations south of Sines.

### 310. Rook *Corvus frugilegus*

A very rare vagrant from other European countries. Only two records are known from the last 50 years: one at Serra do Marão, which involved breeding, and another one in the

Algarve, in 1987. The Rook was reportedly a common winter visitor until the beginning of the 20th century.

## 311. Carrion Crow *Corvus corone*

C A common resident which occurs over most of the country and is especially abundant in the Tagus basin and in certain areas of western central Portugal; it is rare in the Algarve and in the eastern part of Baixo Alentejo, broadly corresponding to the basin of the River Guadiana.

## 312. Hooded Crow *Corvus cornix*

Until recently this crow was considered a subspecies of the Carrion Crow. Isolated birds have been recorded at Vila do Conde in November 2010, December 2011, and October 2013. Another individual was seen on several occasions near Sintra during the second half of 2016. Finally, in July 2019 one bird was found at Cape Espichel and stayed for several weeks. The origin of these birds remains unclear and might be reassessed in the future.

## 313. Northern Raven *Corvus corax*

An uncommon resident which occurs mostly inland, being quite rare near the coast. More frequent in the Alto Alentejo and Beira Interior regions than elsewhere.

## 314. Bohemian Waxwing *Bombycilla garrulus*

One was shot at Anadia in the winter of 1965-66.

## 315. Coal Tit *Periparus ater*

C A common resident, which favours coniferous woodlands, although it also occurs in other types of trees. It is mainly a bird of northern and central Portugal and is particularly abundant in the northwest. South of the Tagus, it is a scarce bird, although small pockets are known to exist in the Serra de São Mamede and in the Setúbal peninsula.

### 316. European Crested Tit *Lophophanes cristatus*

U An uncommon resident which occurs all over the country. It is a bird of woodland, showing a marked preference for conifers, hence it is more abundant in the Sado valley and in the region of Pinhal Interior. It is scarce over much of the inner Alentejo, due to the lack of suitable habitat.

### 317. Eurasian Blue Tit *Cyanistes caeruleus*

C An abundant resident which occurs throughout the country. It is particularly abundant in the Ribatejo, Alto Alentejo and Alentejo Litoral regions, and is scarcer in the northwest.

### 318. Great Tit *Parus major*

C An abundant and widespread resident.

### 319. Eurasian Penduline Tit *Remiz pendulinus*

C A regular winter visitor in small numbers, which can be seen mainly between October and March. It is more frequent in coastal areas south of the River Tagus, being much scarcer elsewhere. A few breeding records are known from several places in the Ribatejo and Alentejo provinces, especially in the Elvas area, where breeding has been proved on several occasions.

### 320. Woodlark *Lullula arborea*

C A common and widespread resident which is particularly abundant in the eastern part of the country lying north of the Tagus and also in the northern part of the Alentejo. It is scarce in the western part of northern and central Portugal.

## 321. Eurasian Skylark *Alauda arvensis*

An uncommon resident and an abundant winter visitor. During the breeding season, it can be found mainly in the highlands of northern and central Portugal, locally also in the plains of the lower River Tagus and along the southwest coast. From October to March, wintering birds can be found throughout the country and are numerous in all types of open ground.

## 322. Thekla's Lark *Galerida theklae*

A common resident, which occurs over most of Algarve, Alentejo, Beira Interior and a large part of the northeast. It is more frequent in the areas lying close to the Spanish border, especially in the south-eastern part of Alentejo, corresponding to the southernmost sector of the Guadiana basin.

## 323. Crested Lark *Galerida cristata*

A common resident, which is widespread south of the River Tagus, although its distribution area has some gaps in south-eastern Alentejo. It also occurs in Beira Interior and, less frequently, along the coast north of Lisbon and in the northern part of the country.

## 324. Greater Short-toed Lark *Calandrella brachydactyla*

An uncommon summer visitor which occurs over most of the territory, although it is rare in the coastal provinces of northern and central Portugal. The regions where it can be found most frequently are the Algarve, Baixo Alentejo, Beira Baixa and certain parts of the northeast. It occurs mainly from late March to late September.

### 325. Calandra Lark *Melanocorypha calandra*

An uncommon resident which occurs mainly in the inner centre and south, locally also in the northeast. It is more frequent in the open plains of the Alentejo.

### 326. Dupont's Lark *Chersophilus duponti*

The only known record involves five birds caught at Alfeite, near Almada, in the 19th century. These specimens were kept in the Bocage Museum, Lisbon, which was unfortunately destroyed by fire in 1978.

### 327. Lesser Short-toed Lark *Alaudala rufescens*

A rare resident which occurs only in the eastern Algarve, namely at the Castro Marim reserve and in some barrier islands of Ria Formosa. Its breeding population comprises a few tens of pairs. Very rarely reported from other places in the Algarve.

### 328. Sand Martin *Riparia riparia*

A common summer visitor which breeds mainly in the western half of Portugal, except in the Algarve where it is chiefly a passage migrant. Usually occurs from February to September, with a few records outside this period.

### 329. Barn Swallow *Hirundo rustica*

An abundant and widespread summer visitor. It arrives in January in the south and from February onwards elsewhere and leaves for Africa in August and September. Occasionally it is seen during the last quarter of the year. Winter roosts have been sporadically recorded at coastal locations.

## 330. Eurasian Crag Martin *Ptyonoprogne rupestris*

Resident or partially migratory, this hirundine is widespread but generally uncommon. It is present in the country throughout the year. Its breeding distribution is expanding and currently covers much of the north and centre and also in the inner south. During the cold season, it is more frequently recorded near the coastline, away from known breeding areas, and it can form large winter roosts with hundreds of birds.

## 331. Common House Martin *Delichon urbicum*

A common summer visitor which breeds all over the country. It occurs mainly from February to October, with a few isolated recorded during the winter.

## 332. Red-rumped Swallow *Cecropis daurica*

An uncommon summer visitor which occurs throughout the country but is rather scarce in the western half to the north of the River Tagus. It is more numerous in the eastern parts of Alentejo and Algarve than elsewhere. It usually arrives in late February and leaves until October, with a few records during the winter period.

## 333. Cetti's Warbler *Cettia cetti*

A common and widespread resident. Its abundance varies markedly between regions: this warbler is more frequent in Ribatejo, over certain parts of Estremadura and in Beira Interior, but it is quite scarce in the northwest and in the Baixo Alentejo. In certain parts of the northwest coast, it seems to occur as a winter visitor only.

## 334. Long-tailed Tit *Aegithalos caudatus*

A common and widespread resident which can be found throughout the country and is more numerous north of the

85

River Tagus and in certain inland areas of the Algarve province. Birds from southern regions (*A. c. irbii*) show a grey mantle and are markedly different from their northern counterparts (*A. c. taiti*), which have a black mantle.

### 335. Wood Warbler *Phylloscopus sibilatrix*

A rare vagrant or perhaps a regular passage migrant in very small numbers. About 23 records are known, most of them in April, May, and September.

### 336. Western Bonelli's Warbler *Phylloscopus bonelli*

An uncommon summer visitor, which breeds mainly in the highlands of northern and central Portugal, where it is locally common, and in the Ribatejo province. Elsewhere it is scarce and occurs chiefly on migration. Can be seen mainly between April and September, with occasional records at other times of the year.

### 337. Hume's Leaf Warbler *Phylloscopus humei*

One seen and photographed at Sagres, Vila do Bispo, in October 2015.

### 338. Yellow-browed Warbler *Phylloscopus inornatus*

A rare passage migrant, which occurs mainly during the post-breeding migration. Up to 2012 about 15 records were known. However, from 2013 onwards this species has been recorded more frequently, with many records throughout the country, almost all of them in October and November. There are a few records from the first four months of the year, possibly referring to overwintering individuals.

## 339. Pallas's Leaf Warbler *Phylloscopus proregulus*

There are four records of this species, of which three in the Algarve and one at Cape Espichel. All birds were seen between late November and late December.

## 340. Dusky Warbler *Phylloscopus fuscatus*

A rare vagrant, which has been recorded on 13 occasions, mostly during the last quarter. Four records come from the Algarve, seven from the Tagus estuary, one from Cape Espichel, and the last one from the Tornada marsh, Caldas da Rainha. One individual was trapped and ringed at the Tagus estuary in May 2016 and was retrapped at the same location in December of the same year, proving that it returned to the same wintering area.

## 341. Willow Warbler *Phylloscopus trochilus*

A very common passage migrant which is more numerous during post-nuptial passage (from late July to early November) than on the pre-nuptial one (March and April).

## 342. Common Chiffchaff *Phylloscopus collybita*

An abundant winter visitor, which is most numerous in coastal lowlands. It occurs in the country mainly from October to March. Singing males have been recorded at several locations during the breeding season, most often in the highlands; these records suggest that a small breeding population may exist.

## 343. Iberian Chiffchaff *Phylloscopus ibericus*

A common summer visitor, which occurs over most of the country, although its distribution shows some discontinuities, especially in the centre and in the southeast, where it may be absent in some areas. The species is more frequent in the provinces of Ribatejo and Estremadura, on the coastal strip south of the Tagus and in the extreme north. It occurs mainly between late February and September.

### 344. Arctic Warbler *Phylloscopus borealis*

Two records are known: a bird was trapped and ringed at Santo André lagoon, in September 2009 and one was seen at Salgados lagoon, Silves, in October 2016.

### 345. Great Reed Warbler *Acrocephalus arundinaceus*

An uncommon summer visitor, which occurs mostly in the southern half of Portugal. Can be locally common in the Tagus and Sado basins. In the centre of the country, it is largely coastal in its distribution, whereas in the north it is rare. It occurs from late March to early September, with odd records outside this period.

### 346. Moustached Warbler *Acrocephalus melanopogon*

Six records are known, three of them in the Algarve and the remaining three at coastal locations in the Alentejo. All records took place between October and March. One of the most recent and best documented records involved two males near Vila Real de Santo António – one of the birds stayed in the area for over a month.

### 347. Aquatic Warbler *Acrocephalus paludicola*

A rare passage migrant that is hard to see due to its elusive habits. It has only been recorded on post-nuptial passage. Most records were made at coastal wetlands and refer mainly to birds caught in mist nets during ringing sessions. Its period of occurrence extends from August to October, with a peak between mid-August and mid-September.

## 348. Sedge Warbler *Acrocephalus schoenobaenus*

An uncommon passage migrant which can be seen during both the pre-nuptial passage, from mid-February to April, and the post-nuptial one, from mid-July to October. It has been recorded over most of the country and seems to be more common in coastal wetlands and in rice fields, but its shy habits make detection difficult.

## 349. Paddyfield Warbler *Acrocephalus agricola*

Seven records are known, all from coastal locations. Most of them took place between August and November, but there is also a record in February.

## 350. Blyth's Reed Warbler *Acrocephalus dumetorum*

First recorded in 2016, with two records, both in October: one of a bird seen near Cape St. Vincent and the second one just a few days later involving a bird trapped during a ringing session near Vila Nova de Milfontes, Odemira.

## 351. Eurasian Reed Warbler *Acrocephalus scirpaceus*

Uncommon as a summer visitor and common on passage. It occurs mainly in the western half of the country, but sometimes it is also found at certain places in the eastern Alentejo. It is usually seen between mid-March and early November.

## 352. African Reed Warbler *Acrocephalus baeticatus*

An uncommon summer visitor. The taxonomy of the Iberian populations is not very clear – they used to be included in the previous species, but according to some recent works, the birds breeding in the Iberian Peninsula belong to the subspecies *ambiguus* of the African Reed Warbler. It should, however, be noted that this change is somewhat controversial and may be reversed in the future.

### 353. Booted Warbler *Iduna caligata*

One seen and photographed near Cape St. Vincent in October 2015 and another one at the Sado estuary in October 2019.

### 354. Western Olivaceous Warbler *Iduna opaca*

A very rare summer visitor, which may not occur regularly. Its distribution area is poorly known. Most records are from the basin of the River Guadiana, especially in the Elvas area, with scattered records from other locations in southern Portugal. The existing records range from early May until October.

### 355. Melodious Warbler *Hippolais polyglotta*

C A common summer migrant which breeds throughout the country and occurs chiefly from mid-April to mid-September. It is especially common along the basin of the River Tagus, and also in the western Alentejo and in the northeast, but it is quite scarce along the basin of the River Guadiana.

### 356. Icterine Warbler *Hippolais icterina*

A very rare vagrant, which has been recorded on four occasions only. There are two autumn records (September or October) and two spring records, both in May.

### 357. Common Grasshopper Warbler *Locustella naevia*

U An uncommon passage migrant, which is recorded mainly on post-nuptial passage, from August to October. Rare during the pre-nuptial migration, with a few records in March and April. Very hard to detect because of its shy habits.

## 358. Savi's Warbler *Locustella luscinioides*

A rare and localized summer visitor. It can only be found at coastal wetlands with large reed beds. The main area for this species lies in the central part of the country, between the rivers Vouga and Mondego, but there are other pockets along the coast, from Minho in the north to the Algarve in the south. Only rarely recorded on migration away from breeding areas.

## 359. Zitting Cisticola *Cisticola juncidis*

A common and widespread resident, which is more abundant in coastal lowlands, particularly in the Ribatejo, Estremadura and Alentejo provinces. It becomes scarcer at a higher altitude and can be considered rare above the 800m level, thus it is absent from much of Trás-os-Montes and certain parts of Beira Interior.

## 360. Eurasian Blackcap *Sylvia atricapilla*

An abundant resident and winter visitor. During the breeding season, it is more common north of the River Tagus, especially in the north and along the coast, but it becomes increasingly scarce as one moves south and east and it is largely absent from much of the inner Alentejo. In winter, it is very abundant in the south, even in places where it does not breed.

## 361. Garden Warbler *Sylvia borin*

An uncommon summer visitor, which breeds only the highlands of northern Portugal, particularly in the Alto Minho and in the northern part of Trás-os-Montes (areas of Barroso and Terra Fria). It is also a very common passage migrant, which occurs throughout the country, mainly between August and October, sometimes as late as November. On pre-nuptial passage it is scarce, with most records in April and May.

### 362. Lesser Whitethroat *Sylvia curruca*

Seven records are known from the last 25 years at various locations in southern Portugal. Most sightings took place in October. Furthermore, there are old references suggesting that this species was to be found in Portugal, but this situation is poorly documented.

### 363. Western Orphean Warbler *Sylvia hortensis*

An uncommon summer visitor, which breeds chiefly in the eastern half of Portugal, from Trás-os-Montes south to the Algarve. It seems to be more abundant in the northeast, chiefly around the International Douro, than elsewhere. It is usually present between April and August and is rarely recorded on passage.

### 364. Common Whitethroat *Sylvia communis*

A locally common summer visitor, which breeds mostly in the highlands of northern and central Portugal, where it occurs from April to August. It is more numerous in the far north and in certain parts of Beira Alta. It also breeds at the peak of Serra de Monchique. Birds on migration turn up in other parts of the country, more often on post-nuptial passage, especially in September, than on the pre-nuptial one.

### 365. Dartford Warbler *Sylvia undata*

A locally common resident which occurs over most of the country, although it is scarce in much of the Alentejo province. It is more abundant in the highlands of northern and central Portugal and in certain areas of the Algarve. Most often found in scrub-covered areas. During the cold season, it is regularly recorded in areas where it does not breed, namely in coastal lowlands.

## 366. Spectacled Warbler *Sylvia conspicillata*

This is an uncommon breeding migrant, which has a patchy distribution. It occurs mostly over the eastern half, but also breeds locally near the coast. Favours dry areas with low scrub. Its main period of occurrence ranges from late February to early November, with very few winter records.

## 367. Subalpine Warbler *Sylvia cantillans*

A summer visitor which occurs in Portugal from March to October. The main areas in which to find this species lie in the inner north and centre, where it is common; can also be found in smaller numbers at certain places in the inner Alentejo and Algarve. When on passage it is regularly recorded near the coast.

## 368. Sardinian Warbler *Sylvia melanocephala*

A common resident, which is more abundant in the southern half of the country. To the north of the River Mondego it is less frequent, especially in the highlands and it can be absent in certain areas of the Trás-os-Montes and Beira Alta provinces.

## 369. Common Firecrest *Regulus ignicapilla*

An uncommon resident and winter visitor. As a breeding bird, it occurs mainly north of the River Tagus, and it is more abundant in the highlands. It also breeds in the south, in small numbers. During the winter months, it is widespread and can be seen throughout the country.

## 370. Goldcrest *Regulus regulus*

A rare winter visitor, which occurs mainly between November and March. It seems to be more frequent in the northern half of the country, but there are also several records in the south. In the winters of 2012-2013 and 2015-

2016, the number of sightings was unusually high, suggesting that small influxes took place.

### 371. Eurasian Wren *Troglodytes troglodytes*

A common and widespread resident. It is particularly common in the north and west, its abundance dropping as one moves south and east. The basin of the River Guadiana, in the southeast, holds the lowest densities.

### 372. Eurasian Nuthatch *Sitta europaea*

A common resident which occurs throughout the country. It is more numerous in Ribatejo and over most of the Alentejo than elsewhere. It is scarce in coastal regions north of the River Tagus and also in the lower basin of the River Guadiana, in the southeast.

### 373. Wallcreeper *Tichodroma muraria*

A very rare winter visitor. Several records are known, most of them between October and March. The species has been recorded at several places, both coastal and inland, usually around cliffs. The place with the highest number of sightings is the Barragem de Santa Luzia, Pampilhosa da Serra, where the species has been recorded almost every winter since 2001.

### 374. Short-toed Treecreeper *Certhia brachydactyla*

A common and widespread resident which is frequent all over the country, except in the extreme southeast, where it is scarce.

### 375. Crested Myna *Acridotheres cristatellus*

An uncommon resident, which has been introduced from Asia. It occurs mainly in the Lisbon region, where it has been expanding – its present distribution comprises the southern strip of the capital along the River Tagus, the Estoril coast and a large part of the Setúbal peninsula. Only rarely recorded elsewhere.

## 376. Rosy Starling *Pastor roseus*

About 45 records are known, referring either to single birds or to groups of two or three. Almost all sightings refer to young birds, mostly seen in September, October, and November. However, there are also a few spring records, suggesting that some birds may have overwintered in the country. The place with most sightings is Cape Espichel (almost half of all records), the remaining ones come from various locations in central and southern Portugal, most of them near the coast.

## 377. Common Starling *Sturnus vulgaris*

A common winter visitor which can be seen mainly between October and February. It seems to be slightly more numerous north of the River Tagus, however, its distribution area and its abundance are masked, due to confusion with the Spotless Starling, with which it often associates.

## 378. Spotless Starling *Sturnus unicolor*

A common and widespread resident which is especially abundant in the Alentejo and in certain parts of the northeast.

## 379. Grey-cheeked Thrush *Catharus minimus*

A single record is known: a wounded individual was found near Esposende in October 2017.

### 380. Ring Ouzel *Turdus torquatus*

A scarce non-breeding visitor which occurs in Portugal mostly from October to April. Most records are from Serra da Estrela, from the coastal areas of Estremadura and from the Algarve, but sightings are known from other parts of the country.

### 381. Common Blackbird *Turdus merula*

A very numerous resident and winter visitor, which occurs throughout the country. It is generally abundant, except in the treeless plains of the inner Alentejo, where it is scarcer.

### 382. Eyebrowed Thrush *Turdus obscurus*

One at Arrimal, Porto de Mós, in October 1991 is the only known record.

### 383. Fieldfare *Turdus pilaris*

A scarce winter visitor which occurs in Portugal from October to March. It seems to be more regular in the northern half, especially in the highlands, however the number of birds wintering in the country fluctuates markedly between years – hence, in some years the Fieldfare is a rare bird, while in other years it is rather frequent.

### 384. Redwing *Turdus iliacus*

A winter visitor, its abundance can vary markedly from year to year – it can be very common in certain years and rather scarce in other years. It occurs throughout the country and can be seen mainly from mid-October to March, often forming mixed parties with other species of thrush.

## 385. Song Thrush *Turdus philomelos*

An uncommon resident, but an abundant winter visitor. It breeds mostly in the north, although its distribution area has been gradually expanding over the last decades and there are already several breeding records in central Portugal and even close to Lisbon. As a winter visitor, it can be seen throughout the country, between October and April.

## 386. Mistle Thrush *Turdus viscivorus*

An uncommon resident which occurs over most of Portugal, usually in low densities. It is more frequent in the north-eastern part of the country.

## 387. Rufous-tailed Scrub Robin *Cercotrichas galactotes*

A rare summer visitor which breeds mainly in the basin of the River Guadiana, corresponding broadly to the eastern parts of the Alentejo and Algarve provinces. It has also been recorded further north, namely in the basin of the River Tagus, but in that area, it is very rare. Birds on passage are sporadically recorded near the coast. Its main period of occurrence extends from May to August, with very few records outside this period.

## 388. Spotted Flycatcher *Muscicapa striata*

An uncommon summer visitor, which occurs usually in low densities. It is more frequent in the Ribatejo and Alto Alentejo provinces. It is also a passage migrant, which is sometimes common on post-nuptial passage, from August to early November, and uncommon or scarce on pre-nuptial passage, which takes place mainly in April.

## 389. European Robin *Erithacus rubecula*

An abundant resident and winter visitor. Breeds in most of the country lying north of the River Tagus and is particularly numerous in the western half; south of the Tagus it is far less common and is largely restricted to certain Serras, such as those of Arrábida, Monchique and São Mamede, and to the southwest coast, where it favours valleys with trees or scrub. Elsewhere it is mainly a non-breeding visitor, occurring from October to March.

### 390. Bluethroat *Luscinia svecica*

An uncommon passage migrant and winter visitor, which occurs mainly from August to March. Largely coastal in its distribution, mainly around wetlands (with salt marsh or reed beds), it is very scarce inland. Has bred at Serra da Estrela and Serra de Montesinho, but this does not appear to happen regularly.

### 391. Common Nightingale *Luscinia megarhynchos*

A common summer visitor and passage migrant, which occurs in Portugal from late March until late August, sometimes later. It is found throughout the country, but it is infrequent in the northwest.

### 392. Red-flanked Bluetail *Tarsiger cyanurus*

One trapped and killed in Boliqueime, Loulé, in January 2012.

### 393. European Pied Flycatcher *Ficedula hypoleuca*

An abundant passage migrant on post-nuptial migration; it can be seen from late July until early November and is especially numerous in September. Rather scarce on pre-nuptial migration, it is sometimes recorded in early spring, when winds blow from the east. May have bred in the Manteigas area, near Serra da Estrela, in 1920.

## 394. Red-breasted Flycatcher *Ficedula parva*

A vagrant species or possibly a rare passage migrant, which has been sporadically recorded on autumn migration. About twenty records are known, most of them in October and November. Sightings were made at several places along the Portuguese coast and it should be noted that more than half of the records took place either on Berlenga island or in the Algarve. On one occasion, the bird overwintered and stayed until March.

## 395. Black Redstart *Phoenicurus ochruros*

A common resident and winter visitor. North of the River Tagus is has a wide distribution as a breeding species, but south of this river it is rather localised and occurs mainly on coastal cliffs and, locally, in the inner Alentejo. Between October and March, it is widespread in the south and can frequently be found on the plains, away from breeding areas.

## 396. Common Redstart *Phoenicurus phoenicurus*

An uncommon summer visitor and passage migrant. It has a discontinuous distribution, mainly along the eastern half of the country, and seems to be more frequent in Ribatejo and in the Alto Alentejo than elsewhere. On migration, it often turns up in places where it does not breed, particularly along the coast. It usually occurs from March to October.

## 397. Moussier's Redstart *Phoenicurus moussieri*

A very rare vagrant from North Africa. The only existing record refers to a male seen at Sagres, Vila do Bispo, between November 2006 and January 2007.

### 398. Common Rock Thrush *Monticola saxatilis*

A rare summer migrant, which occurs chiefly from late April until September. It breeds in the highlands of northern and central Portugal, usually above 1000m altitude. Birds on passage have occasionally been recorded in the south.

### 399. Blue Rock Thrush *Monticola solitarius*

An uncommon and widespread resident with a rather patchy distribution. It is more frequently found in the eastern half of the country, but it also occurs at certain coastal locations. Tending to favour rocky areas, it also breeds locally in urban areas.

### 400. Whinchat *Saxicola rubetra*

A very rare summer visitor, which breeds only in the highlands in the northern tip of Portugal; it is also an uncommon passage migrant which occurs throughout the country. More frequent during the post-nuptial passage than on the pre-nuptial. The main period of occurrence extends from April to October, with scattered records at other times of the year.

### 401. European Stonechat *Saxicola rubicola*

A common resident which occurs throughout the country. It is particularly abundant in the Alentejo, in Ribatejo and in the northern part of Estremadura. In certain parts of the Algarve, it is apparently a non-breeding visitor.

### 402. Siberian Stonechat *Saxicola maurus*

Four isolated records are known, of which two were at Santo André lagoon, one at Ponta da Atalaia (Aljezur) and one on Berlenga island. All records were made between late October and early November.

### 403. Northern Wheatear *Oenanthe oenanthe*

An uncommon summer visitor, which breeds in the northern half of the country, usually above 800m altitude. The southern limit of its breeding area is at the Serra do Açor. It is also an abundant passage migrant, especially on post-nuptial passage. Its period of occurrence is very long, ranging from mid-March until mid-November.

### 404. Isabelline Wheatear *Oenanthe isabellina*

A single record is known: a male was reported at Peniche in October 2015.

### 405. Desert Wheatear *Oenanthe deserti*

Two records, both referring to single birds: a male at Cape Espichel in November 2008 and a male at the Ave river mouth, Vila do Conde, in December 2011.

### 406. Black-eared Wheatear *Oenanthe hispanica*

An uncommon summer visitor, which occurs mainly in the eastern half of the country. Its distribution area is somewhat discontinuous. It is more frequent in the southern part of Trás-os-Montes and in the eastern Algarve – in these regions it can be locally common. The period of occurrence extends from March to September.

### 407. Black Wheatear *Oenanthe leucura*

This is a rare resident which is only to be found in the inner parts of northern and central Portugal, namely along the upper Douro valley and the International Tagus area. In the Alentejo province, it was known to occur locally until the end of the 20th century, but it is uncertain if the species still occurs in this region.

### 408. White-crowned Wheatear *Oenanthe leucopyga*

One at Ria de Alvor, Portimão, in March 2001.

### 409. White-throated Dipper *Cinclus cinclus*

A scarce resident, which occurs mainly in the inland regions of northern and central Portugal, almost always close to rivers and streams, both in the highlands and at a lower altitude. South of the River Tagus, it is a rare species and its presence seems to be sporadic, although breeding has been proved at Portagem, close to Marvão.

### 410. House Sparrow *Passer domesticus*

A very common and widespread resident. Tends to associate to human presence, therefore it is especially abundant in the western provinces north of the River Tagus.

### 411. Spanish Sparrow *Passer hispaniolensis*

Breeds over much of the inland areas and is common in the Beira Baixa province and in certain parts of the Alentejo. Its colonies can congregate many hundreds of pairs. During winter, it can also be found in coastal wetlands, especially in the southern part of the country.

### 412. Eurasian Tree Sparrow *Passer montanus*

This is an uncommon but widespread resident. Its distribution is almost continuous north of the River Tagus, but is quite patchy further south and the species is absent from much of the eastern Alentejo and from most of the Algarve. It can be found chiefly in rural areas, sometimes near human settlements.

413. Rock Sparrow *Petronia petronia*

An uncommon resident which occurs mostly in the inland areas north of the Tagus and also in the Alentejo - it is more numerous in the latter region. In the Algarve it turns up regularly in autumn and winter.

414. White-winged Snowfinch *Montifringilla nivalis*

A very rare vagrant, which has been recorded on very few occasions: one at Serra do Gerês in August 1976; two at Cape St. Vincent in December 1998 and January 1999; three records at Cape Roca in 2005, 2006 e 2007; and finally one near Amoreira beach, Aljezur, in January and February 2016.

415. Black-headed Weaver *Ploceus melanocephalus*

A scarce and localised resident. This weaver is native to the Afrotropics, and it was introduced in the country during the 1990s. It occurs mostly at small marshes, usually with reedbeds or other types of emergent vegetation. The species is known to occur in three different areas: the basin of the lower Tagus, the Tornada marsh (Caldas da Rainha) and the central part of the Algarve.

416. Yellow-crowned Bishop *Euplectes afer*

An uncommon and localised resident. This bird, which is native to Africa, was probably introduced during the second half of the 1980s. It is known to occur at several places near the coast in central and southern Portugal, locally also in the inner Alentejo. Most sightings are made near wetlands. The largest concentrations have been recorded in the Tagus plains.

### 417. Common Waxbill *Estrilda astrild*

A common resident, which is native to sub-Saharan Africa. It was introduced in Portugal in the 1960s. Currently, it can be found over most of the country and is most abundant in coastal lowlands. It is, however, rather scarce in the eastern half and is almost absent from the highlands of the north and centre.

### 418. Red Avadavat *Amandava amandava*

A scarce introduced resident, which originates from Asia. It has a very discontinuous distribution. Its presence has been recorded at several coastal locations, from Minho to the Algarve. It seems to be more frequent in the Tagus basin, including along its tributary the Sorraia, and also in the Alto Alentejo, around Elvas – flocks of several hundred birds have been seen at the last-named site.

### 419. Scaly-breasted Munia *Lonchura punctulata*

A scarce introduced resident. Several young birds were caught at Ria de Alvor, Portimão, in the autumns of 1999 and 2000. Bred at the Boquilobo marsh in October 2000 and eight birds were seen there in July 2002. Several records are known from the Alcácer do Sal area from 2006 onwards, with records of more than 100 birds in 2016. In that year, there were breeding records at several places in the Ribatejo. Isolated records exist from other places in southern Portugal, so it seems that this non-native species is expanding at a fast pace.

### 420. Pin-tailed Whydah *Vidua macroura*

This exotic bird has been recorded several times near coastal wetlands in northern and central Portugal and in the Lisbon region from 2000 onwards. Most sightings are from the Aveiro area, but there was also a record of 50 birds at Barrinha de Mira, Mira, in April 2002. In recent years, this bird has also been regularly recorded in the Ribatejo province. This species is a parasite and lays its eggs on other birds' nests. Its main host is the Common Waxbill.

## 421. Alpine Accentor *Prunella collaris*

A rare but regular winter visitor, which is present mainly from October to March. It has a localised distribution and occurs only at specific locations, usually near cliffs, both coastal and inland. The Serra da Estrela and the castle of Marvão are two places where it seems to be more frequent, but even there it is usually seen in small numbers only.

## 422. Dunnock *Prunella modularis*

An uncommon resident and winter visitor. It breeds in Minho, Douro Litoral, the northern part of Trás-os-Montes and in the main Serras of central Portugal. It can be locally common in scrub areas in the highlands. From October to March, it is also found over the rest of the country.

## 423. Western Yellow Wagtail *Motacilla flava*

A summer visitor which occurs mostly at coastal wetlands and also in certain upland areas north of the River Douro. It is generally uncommon, but it can be locally numerous in certain wetlands, such as the Ria de Aveiro or the Tagus estuary. Can turn up on passage at other places away from breeding areas and on these occasions, other subspecies are frequently recorded. It can usually be seen from February to October, but it has also been regularly recorded in winter, in small numbers.

## 424. Eastern Yellow Wagtail *Motacilla tschutschensis*

A rare vagrant which has been recorded four times in the fields near Vila Franca de Xira. All records took place after

2016 during the wintering period (between November and February).

### 425. Citrine Wagtail *Motacilla citreola*

Seven records are known, all referring to singletons: one at Santo André lagoon, one near Aveiro, two in the Algarve and three in the Vila Franca de Xira plains. Dates span from September to March. Some records refer to wintering individuals, while others probably refer to birds on migration.

### 426. Grey Wagtail *Motacilla cinerea*

U An uncommon resident which can be found throughout the country. As a breeding bird, its distribution area is somewhat discontinuous, especially in southern Ribatejo and in the Alentejo, but during autumn and winter it becomes more frequent in places where it does not breed; in those areas, it usually occurs from October to March.

### 427. White Wagtail *Motacilla alba*

C A common resident and winter visitor. Breeds commonly to the north of the River Tagus and sparsely further south, but during autumn and winter, it is frequent throughout the country. The race *yarrellii*, from the British Isles, can be seen in small numbers during the winter months. An individual of the race *subpersonata*, which breeds in North Africa, was seen at Mina de São Domingos, Mértola, in July 1995.

### 428. Richard's Pipit *Anthus richardi*

A rare winter visitor which has been recorded annually, albeit in very small numbers. Several tens of records are known of isolated birds or small parties, from various coastal locations. It is very rare inland. This pipit occurs mainly between October and April, with scattered records outside this period.

## 429. Blyth's Pipit *Anthus godlewskii*

Four records are known, all referring to isolated birds: the first at Malhão, Odemira, in March 2003; another on Berlenga island, in October 2010; one at the Tagus estuary in March 2011; and finally one near Sagres, Vila do Bispo, in October 2016.

## 430. Tawny Pipit *Anthus campestris*

An uncommon summer visitor and passage migrant, which breeds in the highlands of northern and central Portugal, locally also in certain open areas in the south and in Beira Baixa; it is present mainly from April to October, but occasionally it has been recorded at other times, even in midwinter.

## 431. Meadow Pipit *Anthus pratensis*

An abundant and widespread non-breeding visitor which occurs in the country from late September to early April.

## 432. Tree Pipit *Anthus trivialis*

A rare summer visitor which breeds only in the highlands in the northern tip of the country. Occasionally it also turns up at Serra da Estrela. It is fairly common on passage, especially during post-nuptial migration, and it can then be seen throughout the country. Its normal period of occurrence ranges from March to October.

## 433. Olive-backed Pipit *Anthus hodgsoni*

A very rare vagrant which was first recorded at Ria de Alvor, Portimão, in November 1994; more recently there were some records of birds on autumn migration at several coastal locations in central and southern Portugal between 2011 and 2019. There are also a few winter records.

### 434. Red-throated Pipit *Anthus cervinus*

A rare vagrant which has been recorded about 80 times. All sightings were of singletons or small parties of up to five birds. Almost all records took place between October and May, but there is also a record in September. Records were made south of the River Tagus or in coastal areas of central Portugal.

### 435. Water Pipit *Anthus spinoletta*

*V* An uncommon winter visitor, which turns up during the cold season, chiefly from October to March, at most coastal wetlands, where it can be locally common. Much less frequent inland, where it occurs near water bodies and also in the Serras. Very rare as a breeding bird, presently known only from the uppermost locations in the Serra de Montesinho. Its breeding population is probably less than five pairs.

### 436. Eurasian Rock Pipit *Anthus petrosus*

A rare but regular winter visitor, for which there are several records of single birds or small parties. Almost all records were made along the coastline and most come from the northern half of the country. There is a concentration of records in the period ranging from November to February, with odd observations from other months.

### 437. Common Chaffinch *Fringilla coelebs*

*C* A very common resident and winter visitor. As a breeding species, it is particularly numerous in the inland regions of northern and central Portugal and is scarcer in the southeast and in Estremadura. During the winter it can also be found in the areas where it is rare or absent during the breeding season.

## 438. Brambling *Fringilla montifringilla*

A rare winter visitor which is usually recorded between October and March, however, its numbers fluctuate markedly between years: the species may be quite frequent in certain years and be virtually absent in other years. During the autumn of 2012, the number of records was unusually high.

## 439. Hawfinch *Coccothraustes coccothraustes*

An uncommon resident with a patchy distribution. North of the River Tagus it is mainly a bird of the inland areas and is more frequent in the eastern part of the Guarda district; south of the above-named river the main areas for it are Ribatejo and the coastal Alentejo, to a lesser extent also the northern Alentejo and the eastern Algarve.

## 440. Eurasian Bullfinch *Pyrrhula pyrrhula*

A scarce resident and winter visitor. Breeds mainly in the highlands in the extreme north of the country, namely in the Minho and Trás-os-Montes provinces, but in recent years there have been several breeding records in central Portugal, including one case near Sintra in 2019. Wintering birds occur throughout the country and can be seen from mid-October to early April.

## 441. Trumpeter Finch *Bucanetes githagineus*

There are five records of isolated birds, seen at several locations in southern Portugal.

### 442. Common Rosefinch *Carpodacus erythrinus*

A very rare vagrant, which has only been recorded on autumn passage: eleven records are known, all between mid-September and early November. Six of them were in the Algarve, which is the region where this bird has been recorded on most occasions.

### 443. European Greenfinch *Chloris chloris*

A common widespread resident. It is more frequent in the western half of the country.

### 444. Twite *Linaria flavirostris*

Only one record: a bird at Mindelo, Vila do Conde, in February 1964.

### 445. Common Linnet *Linaria cannabina*

A widespread resident which is generally common, except in the province of Beira Litoral, where it is scarce.

### 446. Common Redpoll *Acanthis flammea*

A very rare vagrant from Central and Northern Europe, which has been recorded on four occasions: four birds trapped at the Ave river mouth, Vila do Conde, in November 1977; one trapped near Póvoa de Varzim, in November 1985; one seen at Cape Espichel, in November 2004; and finally one near Cape St. Vincent in October 2013.

### 447. Red Crossbill *Loxia curvirostra*

A rare breeding, passage and wintering species. In most years it is very scarce and the few sightings come from the highlands of the northern half; however, in irruption years, numbers surge and Crossbills are then recorded throughout the country, even in coastal lowlands – this was the case in 1990 and 1993. As a breeding bird, it may be regular in certain places in northern and central Portugal.

## 448. European Goldfinch *Carduelis carduelis*

A common resident which is very frequent south of the River Tagus and in the province of Estremadura and less numerous in the northern half of the country, especially in Douro Litoral. Numbers are augmented in winter by birds originating from other European countries.

## 449. Citril Finch *Carduelis citrinella*

Three records at Serra da Estrela in March 1987 and one sighting of two birds at Guadramil, Bragança, in October 1990.

## 450. European Serin *Serinus serinus*

An abundant resident which occurs throughout the country. It is especially numerous in the north and centre and is less frequent in the inland parts of the south, namely in the Baixo Alentejo.

## 451. Eurasian Siskin *Spinus spinus*

This is a widespread winter visitor which can be seen in the country between October and early April. Its abundance shows marked fluctuations between years, and the Siskin is quite common in some years and rather scarce in others.

## 452. Lapland Longspur *Calcarius lapponicus*

A rare vagrant from Northern Europe. 15 records are known, mostly in October and November, involving single individuals or small flocks of up to six birds. One third of the sightings were made at Cape Espichel, the remaining ones at other coastal locations.

### 453. Snow Bunting *Plectrophenax nivalis*

A rare winter visitor that is recorded almost every year in very small numbers, mainly between October and March, Most records are from coastal sites, such as dunes, capes and river mouths; there are also several records from the very top of Serra da Estrela and a few isolated records at other inland sites.

### 454. Corn Bunting *Emberiza calandra*

An abundant resident. It is widespread in the region south of the River Tagus and is especially frequent in the plains of the Alentejo; further north it is mainly a bird of the eastern half, but it is also found in the province of Estremadura.

### 455. Yellowhammer *Emberiza citrinella*

A rare and very localised breeding species, which occurs only in the far north and is almost entirely restricted to the region of Barroso. Its migratory status remains unclear – it is known that breeding birds leave the breeding areas and it has been suggested that they move to nearby areas at lower altitudes; additionally, it is possible that birds from other countries spend the winter in Portugal.

### 456. Rock Bunting *Emberiza cia*

This bunting is resident, but its distribution is discontinuous. It occurs chiefly north of the River Tagus and is common in many places, especially in the highlands, but is largely absent from coastal areas south of the River Douro; in the southern part of the country it is a scarce bird, which occurs mainly in the hills of the inner Algarve, but small numbers can also be found in the eastern Alentejo and in certain hills in the western part of this region.

### 457. Ortolan Bunting *Emberiza hortulana*

An uncommon summer visitor to the highlands of northern and central Portugal, generally above 800m. It is fairly common at Serra da Estrela. In the breeding areas, it can usually be found between late April and August. Birds on migration are often recorded in autumn in coastal lowlands, mainly in September and October. Rarely seen during the pre-nuptial passage.

### 458. Cirl Bunting *Emberiza cirlus*

An uncommon resident, which occurs over most of the country, however, it is rare in the basin of the River Guadiana and over much of the Algarve. The highest densities occur in the northeast, especially in the plateau of Miranda do Douro.

### 459. Little Bunting *Emberiza pusilla*

A rare vagrant, which has been recorded 25 times. Most records refer to single birds, but there are at least two cases concerning two birds seen together. All but one record were made at coastal locations. Dates range between October and March.

### 460. Rustic Bunting *Emberiza rustica*

Only three records are known, all referring to single birds in the Algarve: the first was in November 1990 at the Ria de Alvor, Portimão, the second one was on the rice fields of Nossa Senhora do Rosário, Lagoa, in December 2008, and the last one near Sagres in February 2018.

### 461. Yellow-breasted Bunting *Emberiza aureola*

Only one record: a juvenile bird was seen at Cape Espichel in September 1996.

### 462. Black-headed Bunting *Emberiza melanocephala*

An adult male was seen in the Vila Franca de Xira plains in June 2018.

### 463. Pallas's Reed Bunting *Emberiza pallasi*

One was recorded at Santo André lagoon in January 1997.

### 464. Common Reed Bunting *Emberiza schoeniclus*

A rare resident and very localised breeding species, which nowadays is almost exclusively restricted to the Minho and Tagus estuaries and the Ria de Aveiro. It is also an uncommon wintering species, which occurs throughout the country, mainly in the western half. Tends to favour wet areas, such as reed beds, marshes and agricultural fields with ditches covered by emergent vegetation.

### 465. Common Yellowthroat *Geothlypis trichas*

A first winter male was trapped and ringed at Vilamoura, Loulé, in October 2010.

# Part Two: Birds of uncertain origin

This section comprises 7 species that have been recorded, for whose wild provenance some doubts remain or cannot now be ascertained. Although they may be genuine vagrants that arrived in the country naturally, the possibility of their being escapes from captivity cannot be excluded.

### 466. Canada Goose *Branta canadensis*

Several records are known from different places, referring to single birds or flocks. Dates range mainly from late September to mid-March, but there is a record in July.

### 467. Mute Swan *Cygnus olor*

About fifty records exist, chiefly from coastal wetlands. Some records refer to small flocks. Sightings were made throughout the year, but two out of every three took place between October and March. May have bred at some reservoirs in the Alentejo in recent years, but in some cases, the birds were probably introduced.

### 468. Laughing Dove *Spilopelia senegalensis*

One was seen at Rebelva, Cascais, in January 1996, and another one was recorded at Mexilhoeira Grande, Portimão, in April 2008.

### 469. Lesser Flamingo *Phoeniconaias minor*

About 20 records are known, invariably involving one or two birds, usually among flocks of Greater Flamingos. The birds were seen in the Mondego and Tagus estuaries or along the Algarve coast. Some birds had rings on them, revealing that they were of captive origin.

### 470. Great White Pelican *Pelecanus onocrotalus*

There are nine records, scattered throughout the country from different times of the year. Two of them involved two birds; all other records refer to singletons.

### 471. Steppe Eagle *Aquila nipalensis*

A single bird was seen in the Lezíria Grande, Vila Franca de Xira, in July 2015. The following month, an individual, possibly the same, was seen in the plains of Castro Verde, and regular sightings of this bird took place in the same area until at least August 2016. In October 2016, a bird was seen at Sagres – it came from Spain and was certainly an escape. In 2018 and 2019 there were more sightings in the Castro Verde region.

### 472. Gyrfalcon *Falco rusticolus*

One was seen on the southwest coast in March 1991.

# Part Three: Non-native birds

This section comprises a list of 22 non-native bird species that have been observed in the wild in mainland Portugal which have bred in the wild but for which no self-sustaining populations are known. Species for which breeding is believed to have taken place are also included.

### 473. Helmeted Guineafowl *Numida meleagris*

Four birds (two adults and two chicks) at Cernache, Coimbra, in May 2012.

### 474. Common Pheasant *Phasianus colchicus*

There are many sightings of pheasants throughout the country, referring to birds released for hunting purposes. Breeding in the wild has been frequently recorded, but no sustainable populations are known to exist.

### 475. Muscovy Duck *Cairina moschata*

Bred near the Cabril dam, Pedrógão Grande, in 2004. Several sightings were made later in the Zêzere valley and also at the Cávado estuary and at several locations in the Alentejo, with a record of two females with young birds at Mourão, in May 2006.

### 476. Common Ground Dove *Columbina passerina*

A breeding record in Évora, in 1998, involving seven birds that escaped from captivity. The species later disappeared from the area.

### 477. African Sacred Ibis *Threskiornis aethiopicus*

There is a breeding record from the lower Mondego in 1998, involving birds that had escaped from a nearby zoo; in that year, a maximum of six birds were seen by late summer. Since 2008 there have been several records of birds in the wild in other parts of the country, mainly in the Algarve, but also in the Tagus and Sado estuaries.

### 478. Grey Parrot *Psittacus erithacus*

There are several records in the wild. The most recent ones were in Coimbra in 2005, then at Caldas da Rainha in May 2010 (in this case a pair was seen building a nest), another at Cape Espichel in September 2010 and finally one at Cruz Quebrada, Oeiras, in January 2014.

### 479. Senegal Parrot *Poicephalus senegalus*

Many records in Lisbon, from 1998 onwards. Most sightings were made in public parks located in the central or western parts of the city, involving singletons or small flocks of up to ten birds. In December 2012 six were seen at Algés, at the western end of the city.

### 480. Monk Parakeet *Myiopsitta monachus*

There are several records of this species throughout the country, from 1996 onwards. In most cases, singles or groups of two birds were seen, but there was a party of 16 in Porto, in April 2016, and there are recent records in this city. Has bred in the Porto and Lisbon areas and also in the Algarve.

## 481. Blue-crowned Parakeet *Thectocercus acuticaudatus*

Several birds were seen at Jardim da Estrela, Lisbon, in October and November 1998. There are many other records from Lisbon and in the surrounding areas, from 2005 onwards, both of single birds and of small flocks of up to 45 individuals in public parks and gardens. In 2008 there were also two records of single birds at Herdade da Mitra, Évora and a record of two birds in Ludo, Faro.

## 482. Budgerigar *Melopsittacus undulatus*

There are several sightings of single birds throughout the country. Additionally, there is a breeding record from Coruche in the mid-1990s, when seven birds were released and bred in the wild; the population quickly reached 100 birds, but after that, the local inhabitants exterminated them.

## 483. Fischer's Lovebird *Agapornis fischeri*

Breeds locally in the Algarve, mainly between Carvoeiro (Lagoa) and Armação de Pera (Silves). The population seems to be expanding, but its size is unknown.

## 484. Red-billed Leiothrix *Leiothrix lutea*

Several records exist of single birds or small flocks, many of them in the Estremadura province. The place with most sightings is the Serra de Sintra, where small parties have been regularly recorded but less so in recent years. Additionally, there have been records in the Beira Litoral, namely at Serra da Lousã, where this species could be on its way to becoming self-sustaining, and also in the Algarve.

## 485. Common Myna *Acridotheres tristis*

Regularly observed in Lisbon, especially at Praça do Comércio and in the surrounding areas, from 2001 until at least 2017. During the same period, the species was also recorded at several places along the Estoril coast, between Caxias (Oeiras) and Cascais. On the southern bank of the River Tagus, there are several records from 2002 onwards. Finally, there was an isolated record in Porto and another one in Viana do Castelo, both in 2006.

### 486. Village Weaver *Ploceus cucullatus*

Has been recorded in several places in western Portugal, from north to south, often near wetlands. The place with the highest number of records is the Barroca marsh, Alcochete, where the species was regularly seen from 2005 until at least 2010. Breeding was recorded near Benavente in June 2001. An abandoned colony was found near Riachos, Torres Novas, in 1998, suggesting that breeding may have also taken place there.

### 487. Black-winged Red Bishop *Euplectes hordeaceus*

Isolated records are known from the Algarve (it may have bred in Burgau, Lagos, in 1993) and also from the Boquilobo marsh in 2006 and from Cape Espichel in 2007.

### 488. Orange-cheeked Waxbill *Estrilda melpoda*

Several records are known, all from before 2000, at several coastal locations. Two of them refer to actual breeding, with young being fed by adults: in the western Algarve between 1988 and 1992 and then in Lisbon in 1998 (on the latter occasion a maximum of 11 birds were seen together). There are a few more isolated records in the Lisbon area, at Barrinha de Esmoriz (Ovar) and in the Algarve.

### 489. Black-rumped Waxbill *Estrilda troglodytes*

All existing records were made before 2000, mostly in the north (with several records of small flocks in the valleys of the rivers Minho and Lima) and in the Algarve. Additionally, a bird was ringed near Coimbra in the 1970s.

## 490. Orange-breasted Waxbill *Amandava subflava*

Regularly recorded in the Caniceiras marsh, Loures, during summer and autumn 1998, with a maximum of 16 birds seen. Also recorded in other places, including a case of a female trapped at the Santo André lagoon in September 2000 and three birds caught in the Taipal marsh, Montemor-o-Velho, in September 2003.

## 491. Zebra Finch *Taeniopygia guttata*

There is a record involving 16 birds in the Algarve, namely in the valley of the River Arade, Silves, where the species may have bred in the wild during the 1980s. In the following decade, there were several records of one or two birds at sites in central Portugal. More recently (from 2007 onwards) there was a record near Caldas da Rainha, two isolated records near Porto and one in the Algarve.

## 492. African Silverbill *Euodice cantans*

A few records exist from the 1990s at the Barrinha de Esmoriz, Ovar, involving small numbers.

## 493. Chestnut Munia *Lonchura atricapilla*

This species has been recorded mainly in the district of Setúbal, especially in the Sado estuary and in the area of Alcochete; at these sites, flocks of several tens of birds were seen in the past. This species has also been seen at Albufeira lagoon in 2002, with isolated records from a few other places, namely in the Algarve and at coastal locations in northern and central Portugal. However, there are few recent sightings and therefore the current status of this bird in the country cannot be ascertained. The introduced population may have disappeared.

## 494. White-headed Munia *Lonchura maja*

May have bred in the River Arade, Silves, in the early 1990s. During that same decade, a few birds were caught at the Santo André lagoon. Finally, two adults and a young bird were seen at Rilvas, Alcochete, in April 2002.

# Bibliography

Aves de Portugal – o portal dos observadores de aves. Available online at: http://www.avesdeportugal.info. Viewed 3 January 2020.

BirdLife - www.birdlife.org – official site of BirdLife International

British Ornithologists' Union. *Species categories*. Available online at: http://www.bou.org.uk/british-list/species-categories/ - official site of the British Ornithologists' Union. Viewed 3 January 2020.

Catry, P., Costa, H., Elias, G. & Matias, R. (2010). *Aves de Portugal. Ornitologia do território continental*. Assírio & Alvim, Lisboa.

Costa, H. & Comité Português de Raridades da SPEA 1997. Aves de ocorrência rara ou acidental em Portugal. Relatório do Comité Português de Raridades referente ao ano de 1995. *Pardela* 5: 4-19.

Costa, H. & Farinha, J. C. (compil.) 1994. Lista das observações de aves de ocorrência rara ou acidental homologadas pelo Comité Ibérico de Raridades. *Airo* 5: 37-40.

Costa, H. & Farinha, J. C. (compil.) 1995. Lista de observações de aves de ocorrência rara ou acidental em Portugal, homologadas pelo Comité Ibérico de Raridades. *Airo* 6: 76-79.

Costa, H. & Farinha, J. C. (compil.) 1996. Lista das observações de aves de ocorrência rara ou acidental em Portugal homologadas pelo Comité Ibérico de Raridades. *Airo* 7 (2): 96-98.

Costa, H., Bolton, M., Catry, P., Gordinho, L. & Moore, C. C. 1999a. Aves de ocorrência rara ou acidental em Portugal. Relatório do Comité Português de Raridades referente ao ano de 1996. *Pardela* 8: 3-23.

Costa, H., Bolton, M., Catry, P., Matias, R., Moore, C. C. & Tomé, R. 2000b. Aves de ocorrência rara ou acidental em Portugal. Relatório do Comité Português de Raridades referente aos anos de 1997 e 1998. *Pardela* 11: 3-27.

Costa, H., Bolton, M., Matias, R., Moore, C. C. & Tomé, R. 2003. Aves de ocorrência rara ou acidental em Portugal. Relatório do Comité Português de Raridades referente aos anos de 1999, 2000 e 2001. *Anuário Ornitológico* 1: 3-35.

Elias, G., Costa, H., Matias, R., Moore, C. C. & Tomé, R. 2004. Aves de ocorrência rara ou acidental em Portugal. Relatório do Comité Português de Raridades referente ao ano de 2002. *Anuário Ornitológico* 2: 1-20.

Elias, G., Costa, H., Matias, R., Moore, C. C. & Tomé, R. 2005. Aves de ocorrência rara ou acidental em Portugal. Relatório do Comité Português de Raridades referente ao ano de 2003. *Anuário Ornitológico* 3: 1-22.

Elias, G., Costa, H., Matias, R., Moore, C. C. & Tomé, R. 2006. Aves de ocorrência rara ou acidental em Portugal. Relatório do Comité Português de Raridades referente ao ano de 2004. *Anuário Ornitológico* 4: 1-16.

Equipa Atlas 2008. *Atlas das Aves Nidificantes em Portugal (1999-2005)*. Instituto da Conservação da Natureza, Sociedade Portuguesa para o Estudo das Aves, Parque Natural da Madeira e Secretaria Regional do Ambiente e do Mar. Assírio & Alvim, Lisboa.

Farinha, J. C. & Costa, H. 1993. Lista de observações de aves de ocorrência rara ou acidental em Portugal, homologadas pelo Comité Ibérico de Raridades. *Airo* 4: 34-37.

Farinha, J. C. (Compil.) 1991c. Lista das observações de aves efectuadas em Portugal, aceites pelo Comité Ibérico de Raridades. *Airo* 2: 25-27.

Gill, F & Donsker, D. (Eds). 2019. IOC World Bird List (v9.2). doi: 10.14344/IOC.ML.9.2. Available online at:. https://www.worldbirdnames.org/. Viewed 3 January 2020.

Jara, J., Alfrey, P., Costa, H., Matias, R., Moore, C. C., Santos, J. L. & Tipper, R. Relatório do Comité Português de Raridades referente aos anos de 2008 e 2009. *Anuário Ornitológico* 7: 3-71.

Jara, J., Costa, H., Elias, G., Matias, R., Moore, C.C. & Tomé, R. 2007. Aves de ocorrência rara ou acidental em Portugal. Relatório do Comité Português de Raridades referente ao ano de 2005. *Anuário Ornitológico* 5: 1-34.

Jara, J., Costa, H., Matias, R., Moore, C. C., Noivo, C. & Tipper, R. 2009. Aves de ocorrência rara ou acidental em Portugal. *Anuário Ornitológico* 6: 1-45.

Matias, R. & Lobo, F. 1999. *Aves exóticas que nidificam em Portugal Continental.* Unpublished report. SPEA, Lisboa.

Matias, R. (Comp.) 2003. Aves exóticas em Portugal: anos de 2000 e 2001. *Anuário Ornitológico* 1: 47-51.

Matias, R. (Comp.) 2004. Aves exóticas em Portugal: ano de 2002. *Anuário Ornitológico* 2: 55-63.

Matias, R. (Comp.) 2006a Aves exóticas em Portugal: anos de 2003 e 2004. *Anuário Ornitológico* 4: 55-63.

Matias, R. 2002. *Aves Exóticas que Nidificam em Portugal Continental.* Instituto da Conservação da Natureza, Lisboa.

Matias, R. 2009-10. Aves exóticas em Portugal: anos de 2005-2008. *Anuário Ornitológico* 7: 95-108. Available online at: http://www.spea.pt/fotos/editor2/spea_anuario_ornitologico_a ves_exoticas_em_portugal_2005_2008_p95_108.pdf. Viewed Viewed 3 January 2020.

Matias, R. 2011. Aves exóticas em Portugal: anos de 2009 e 2010. *Anuário Ornitológico* 8: 94-104. Available online at: http://www.spea.pt/fotos/editor2/anuario_ornitologico8_3.pdf. Viewed Viewed 3 January 2020.

Matias, R., Catry, P., Costa, H., Elias, G., Jara, J, Moore, C.C. & Tomé, R. 2007. Lista sistemática das aves de Portugal Continental. *Anuário Ornitológico* 5: 74-132.

Matias, R., Alfrey, P., Crochet, P.-A-, Gonçalves, A., Jara, J., Mitchell, D., Moore, C. C., Muchaxo, J., Santos, J. L., Tavares, J. T. & Tipper, R. 2012. Aves de ocorrência rara ou acidental em Portugal. Relatório do Comité Português de Raridades referente ao ano de 2011. *Anuário Ornitológico* 9: 3-56

Matias, R., Alfrey, P., Crochet, P.-A., Gonçalves, A., Mitchell, D., Tavares, J. T. & Tipper, R. 2018. Aves de ocorrência rara ou acidental em Portugal. Relatório do Comité Português de Raridades referente ao ano de 2012. *Anuário Ornitológico* 10: 3-66.

Muchaxo, J., Alfrey, P., Costa, H., Jara, J., Matias, R., Moore, C. C., Santos, J. L. & Tipper, R. Aves de ocorrência rara ou acidental em Portugal. Relatório do Comité Português de Raridades referente ao ano de 2010. *Anuário Ornitológico* 8: 3-52.

Petronilho, J. M. S., J. V. Vingada & J. Ferreira 2004. As aves exóticas na costa de Quiaios-Mira (Beira Litoral, Portugal). *Airo* 14: 114-120.

Reis Júnior, J. A. 1931. *Catálogo Sistemático e Analítico das Aves de Portugal.* Araújo & Sobrinhos e Sucessores, Porto.

Rufino, R. (Coord.) 1989a. *Atlas das Aves que Nidificam em Portugal Continental.* CEMPA / SNPRCN, Lisboa.

# Index

## A

Acanthis flammea, 110
Accipiter gentilis, 70
Accipiter nisus, 69
Acridotheres cristatellus, 94
Acridotheres tristis, 119
Acrocephalus agricola, 89
Acrocephalus arundinaceus, 88
Acrocephalus baeticatus, 89
Acrocephalus dumetorum, 89
Acrocephalus melanopogon, 88
Acrocephalus paludicola, 88
Acrocephalus schoenobaenus, 89
Acrocephalus scirpaceus, 89
Actitis hypoleucos, 43
Actitis macularius, 43
Aegithalos caudatus, 85
Aegypius monachus, 67
African Reed Warbler, 89
African Sacred Ibis, 118
African Silverbill, 121
Agapornis fischeri, 119
Alauda arvensis, 83
Alaudala rufescens, 84
Alca torda, 55
Alcedo atthis, 74
Alectoris rufa, 13
Alle alle, 55
Allen's Gallinule, 29
Alopochen aegyptiaca, 16
Alpine Accentor, 105
Alpine Swift, 24
Amandava amandava, 104
Amandava subflava, 121
American Coot, 30
American Golden Plover, 34
American Herring Gull, 49
American Wigeon, 18

Anas acuta, 18
Anas carolinensis, 18
Anas crecca, 18
Anas platyrhynchos, 18
Anser albifrons, 15
Anser anser, 14
Anser brachyrhynchus, 15
Anser caerulescens, 14
Anser fabalis, 15
Anser serrirostris, 15
Anthus campestris, 107
Anthus cervinus, 108
Anthus godlewskii, 107
Anthus hodgsoni, 107
Anthus petrosus, 108
Anthus pratensis, 107
Anthus richardi, 106
Anthus spinoletta, 108
Anthus trivialis, 107
Apus affinis, 25
Apus apus, 24
Apus caffer, 25
Apus pallidus, 24
Aquatic Warbler, 88
Aquila adalberti, 69
Aquila chrysaetos, 69
Aquila fasciata, 69
Aquila nipalensis, 116
Arctic Tern, 53
Arctic Warbler, 88
Ardea alba, 64
Ardea cinerea, 64
Ardea purpurea, 64
Ardenna gravis, 59
Ardenna grisea, 59
Ardeola ralloides, 63
Arenaria interpres, 37
Asio capensis, 74
Asio flammeus, 73
Asio otus, 73

*Athene noctua*, 73
Atlantic Puffin, 56
Audouin's Gull, 47
*Aythya affinis*, 20
*Aythya collaris*, 20
*Aythya ferina*, 19
*Aythya fuligula*, 20
*Aythya marila*, 20
*Aythya nyroca*, 19

# B

Baillon's Crake, 28
Baird's Sandpiper, 39
Balearic Shearwater, 59
Band-rumped Storm Petrel, 57
Barn Owl, 72
Barn Swallow, 84
Barnacle Goose, 14
Barolo Shearwater, 60
Bar-tailed Godwit, 37
*Bartramia longicauda*, 36
Bearded Vulture, 65
Black Kite, 71
Black Redstart, 99
Black Stork, 60
Black Tern, 54
Black Wheatear, 101
Black-bellied Sandgrouse, 26
Black-browed Albatross, 57
Black-crowned Night Heron, 63
Black-eared Wheatear, 101
Black-headed Bunting, 114
Black-headed Gull, 46
Black-headed Weaver, 103
Black-legged Kittiwake, 45
Black-necked Grebe, 32
Black-rumped Waxbill, 120
Black-tailed Godwit, 37
Black-throated Loon, 56
Black-winged Kite, 65
Black-winged Red Bishop, 120
Black-winged Stilt, 33
Blue Rock Thrush, 100
Blue-crowned Parakeet, 119
Bluethroat, 98
Blue-winged Teal, 17
Blyth's Pipit, 107
Blyth's Reed Warbler, 89

Bohemian Waxwing, 81
*Bombycilla garrulus*, 81
Bonaparte's Gull, 46
Bonelli's Eagle, 69
Booted Eagle, 68
Booted Warbler, 90
*Botaurus stellaris*, 62
Brambling, 109
Brant Goose, 14
*Branta bernicla*, 14
*Branta canadensis*, 115
*Branta leucopsis*, 14
Bridled Tern, 52
Broad-billed Sandpiper, 38
Brown Booby, 61
*Bubo bubo*, 73
*Bubulcus ibis*, 63
*Bucanetes githagineus*, 109
*Bucephala albeola*, 22
*Bucephala clangula*, 22
Budgerigar, 119
Buff-breasted Sandpiper, 40
Bufflehead, 22
Bulwer's Petrel, 60
*Bulweria bulwerii*, 60
*Burhinus oedicnemus*, 32
*Buteo buteo*, 72
*Buteo rufinus*, 72
*Butorides virescens*, 63

# C

*Cairina moschata*, 117
Calandra Lark, 84
*Calandrella brachydactyla*, 83
*Calcarius lapponicus*, 111
*Calidris acuminata*, 38
*Calidris alba*, 39
*Calidris alpina*, 39
*Calidris bairdii*, 39
*Calidris canutus*, 38
*Calidris falcinellus*, 38
*Calidris ferruginea*, 38
*Calidris fuscicollis*, 40
*Calidris himantopus*, 38
*Calidris maritima*, 39
*Calidris melanotos*, 40
*Calidris minuta*, 40
*Calidris pugnax*, 38

*Calidris pusilla*, 40
*Calidris subruficollis*, 40
*Calidris temminckii*, 39
*Calonectris borealis*, 59
*Calonectris diomedea*, 58
Canada Goose, 115
*Caprimulgus europaeus*, 24
*Caprimulgus ruficollis*, 23
*Carduelis carduelis*, 111
*Carduelis citrinella*, 111
*Carpodacus erythrinus*, 110
Carrion Crow, 81
Caspian Gull, 50
Caspian Tern, 51
*Catharus minimus*, 95
*Cecropis daurica*, 85
*Cercotrichas galactotes*, 97
*Certhia brachydactyla*, 94
Cetti's Warbler, 85
*Cettia cetti*, 85
*Chaetura pelagica*, 24
*Charadrius alexandrinus*, 35
*Charadrius dubius*, 35
*Charadrius hiaticula*, 35
*Charadrius mongolus*, 35
*Charadrius morinellus*, 36
*Charadrius vociferus*, 35
*Chersophilus duponti*, 84
Chestnut Munia, 121
Chimney Swift, 24
*Chlidonias hybrida*, 53
*Chlidonias leucopterus*, 53
*Chlidonias niger*, 54
*Chloris chloris*, 110
*Chroicocephalus genei*, 46
*Chroicocephalus philadelphia*, 46
*Chroicocephalus ridibundus*, 46
*Ciconia ciconia*, 60
*Ciconia nigra*, 60
*Cinclus cinclus*, 102
Cinereous Vulture, 67
*Circaetus gallicus*, 68
*Circus aeruginosus*, 70
*Circus cyaneus*, 70
*Circus hudsonius*, 70
*Circus macrourus*, 71
*Circus pygargus*, 71
Cirl Bunting, 113
*Cisticola juncidis*, 91

Citril Finch, 111
Citrine Wagtail, 106
*Clamator glandarius*, 26
*Clanga clanga*, 68
*Clanga pomarina*, 68
*Clangula hyemalis*, 22
Coal Tit, 81
*Coccothraustes coccothraustes*, 109
Collared Pratincole, 45
*Coloeus monedula*, 80
*Columba livia*, 27
*Columba oenas*, 27
*Columba palumbus*, 27
*Columbina passerina*, 118
Common Blackbird, 96
Common Buttonquail, 32
Common Buzzard, 72
Common Chaffinch, 108
Common Chiffchaff, 87
Common Crane, 30
Common Cuckoo, 26
Common Eider, 21
Common Firecrest, 93
Common Goldeneye, 22
Common Grasshopper Warbler, 90
Common Greenshank, 45
Common Ground Dove, 118
Common House Martin, 85
Common Kestrel, 76
Common Kingfisher, 74
Common Linnet, 110
Common Loon, 56
Common Merganser, 22
Common Moorhen, 30
Common Murre, 55
Common Myna, 119
Common Nightingale, 98
Common Pheasant, 117
Common Pochard, 19
Common Quail, 14
Common Redpoll, 110
Common Redshank, 44
Common Redstart, 99
Common Reed Bunting, 114
Common Ringed Plover, 35
Common Rock Thrush, 100
Common Sandpiper, 43
Common Scoter, 21
Common Shelduck, 16

Common Snipe, 41
Common Starling, 95
Common Swift, 24
Common Tern, 52
Common Waxbill, 104
Common Whitethroat, 92
Common Wood Pigeon, 27
Common Yellowthroat, 114
*Coracias garrulus*, 74
Corn Bunting, 112
Corn Crake, 28
*Corvus corax*, 81
*Corvus cornix*, 81
*Corvus corone*, 81
*Corvus frugilegus*, 80
Cory's Shearwater, 59
*Coturnix coturnix*, 14
Cream-coloured Courser, 45
Crested Lark, 83
Crested Myna, 94
*Crex crex*, 28
*Cuculus canorus*, 26
Curlew Sandpiper, 38
*Cursorius cursor*, 45
*Cyanistes caeruleus*, 82
*Cyanopica cooki*, 79
*Cygnus columbianus*, 15
*Cygnus cygnus*, 16
*Cygnus olor*, 115

## D

Dartford Warbler, 92
Delichon urbicum, 85
*Dendrocopos major*, 75
Desert Wheatear, 101
*Diomedea exulans*, 57
*Dryobater minor*, 75
Dunlin, 39
Dunnock, 105
Dupont's Lark, 84
Dusky Warbler, 87

## E

Eastern Yellow Wagtail, 105
*Egretta garzetta*, 64
*Egretta gularis*, 64

Egyptian Goose, 16
Egyptian Vulture, 66
*Elanus caeruleus*, 65
Eleonora's Falcon, 76
*Emberiza aureola*, 114
*Emberiza calandra*, 112
*Emberiza cia*, 112
*Emberiza cirlus*, 113
*Emberiza citrinella*, 112
*Emberiza hortulana*, 113
Emberiza melanocephala, 114
*Emberiza pallasi*, 114
*Emberiza pusilla*, 113
*Emberiza rustica*, 113
*Emberiza schoeniclus*, 114
*Erithacus rubecula*, 97
*Estrilda astrild*, 104
*Estrilda melpoda*, 120
*Estrilda troglodytes*, 120
*Euodice cantans*, 121
*Euplectes afer*, 103
*Euplectes hordeaceus*, 120
Eurasian Bittern, 62
Eurasian Blackcap, 91
Eurasian Blue Tit, 82
Eurasian Bullfinch, 109
Eurasian Collared Dove, 28
Eurasian Coot, 30
Eurasian Crag Martin, 85
Eurasian Curlew, 37
Eurasian Dotterel, 36
Eurasian Eagle-Owl, 73
Eurasian Golden Oriole, 79
Eurasian Hobby, 77
Eurasian Hoopoe, 74
Eurasian Jay, 79
Eurasian Magpie, 80
Eurasian Nuthatch, 94
Eurasian Oystercatcher, 32
Eurasian Penduline Tit, 82
Eurasian Reed Warbler, 89
Eurasian Rock Pipit, 108
Eurasian Scops Owl, 72
Eurasian Siskin, 111
Eurasian Skylark, 83
Eurasian Sparrowhawk, 69
Eurasian Spoonbill, 62
Eurasian Stone-curlew, 32
Eurasian Teal, 18

Eurasian Tree Sparrow, 102
Eurasian Whimbrel, 36
Eurasian Wigeon, 17
Eurasian Woodcock, 41
Eurasian Wren, 94
Eurasian Wryneck, 75
European Bee-eater, 74, 75
European Crested Tit, 82
European Golden Plover, 34
European Goldfinch, 111
European Greenfinch, 110
European Herring Gull, 49
European Honey Buzzard, 66
European Nightjar, 24
European Pied Flycatcher, 98
European Robin, 97
European Roller, 74
European Serin, 111
European Shag, 61
European Stonechat, 100
European Storm Petrel, 57
European Turtle Dove, 27
Eyebrowed Thrush, 96

## F

*Falco biarmicus*, 77
*Falco cherrug*, 77
*Falco columbarius*, 77
*Falco eleonorae*, 76
*Falco naumanni*, 76
*Falco peregrinus*, 77
*Falco rusticolus*, 116
*Falco subbuteo*, 77
*Falco tinnunculus*, 76
*Falco vespertinus*, 76
Fea's Petrel, 58
Ferruginous Duck, 19
*Ficedula hypoleuca*, 98
*Ficedula parva*, 99
Fieldfare, 96
Fischer's Lovebird, 119
Forster's Tern, 53
Franklin's Gull, 47
*Fratercula arctica*, 56
*Fringilla coelebs*, 108
*Fringilla montifringilla*, 109
*Fulica americana*, 30
*Fulica atra*, 30

*Fulica cristata*, 30
*Fulmarus glacialis*, 58

## G

Gadwall, 17
*Galerida cristata*, 83
*Galerida theklae*, 83
*Gallinago delicata*, 42
*Gallinago gallinago*, 41
*Gallinago media*, 41
*Gallinula chloropus*, 30
Garden Warbler, 91
Garganey, 16
*Garrulus glandarius*, 79
*Gavia arctica*, 56
*Gavia immer*, 56
*Gavia stellata*, 56
*Gelochelidon nilotica*, 50
*Geothlypis trichas*, 114
*Glareola pratincola*, 45
Glaucous Gull, 49
Glossy Ibis, 62
Goldcrest, 93
Golden Eagle, 69
Great Black-backed Gull, 48
Great Bustard, 25
Great Cormorant, 61
Great Crested Grebe, 31
Great Egret, 64
Great Reed Warbler, 88
Great Shearwater, 59
Great Skua, 54
Great Snipe, 41
Great Spotted Cuckoo, 26
Great Spotted Woodpecker, 75
Great Tit, 82
Great White Pelican, 116
Greater Flamingo, 32
Greater Scaup, 20
Greater Short-toed Lark, 83
Greater Spotted Eagle, 68
Greater White-fronted Goose, 15
Greater Yellowlegs, 45
Green Heron, 63
Green Sandpiper, 43
Green-winged Teal, 18
Grey Heron, 64
Grey Parrot, 118

Grey Partridge, 13
Grey Plover, 34
Grey Wagtail, 106
Grey-cheeked Thrush, 95
Greylag Goose, 14
Griffon Vulture, 67
*Grus grus*, 30
Gull-billed Tern, 50
*Gypaetus barbatus*, 65
*Gyps africanus*, 66
*Gyps fulvus*, 67
*Gyps rueppellii*, 67
Gyrfalcon, 116

**H**

*Haematopus ostralegus*, 32
*Haliaeetus albicilla*, 72
Hawfinch, 109
Helmeted Guineafowl, 117
Hen Harrier, 70
*Hieraaetus pennatus*, 68
*Himantopus himantopus*, 33
*Hippolais icterina*, 90
*Hippolais polyglotta*, 90
*Hirundo rustica*, 84
Hooded Crow, 81
Horned Grebe, 31
House Sparrow, 102
Hudsonian Whimbrel, 36
Hume's Leaf Warbler, 86
*Hydrobates pelagicus*, 57
*Hydrocoloeus minutus*, 47
*Hydroprogne caspia*, 51

**I**

Iberian Chiffchaff, 87
Iberian Green Woodpecker, 75
Iberian Grey Shrike, 78
Iberian Magpie, 79
Iceland Gull, 49
*Ichthyaetus audouinii*, 47
*Ichthyaetus melanocephalus*, 48
Icterine Warbler, 90
*Iduna caligata*, 90
*Iduna opaca*, 90
Isabelline Wheatear, 101

Ivory Gull, 46
*Ixobrychus minutus*, 62

**J**

Jack Snipe, 41
*Jynx torquilla*, 75

**K**

Kelp Gull, 49
Kentish Plover, 35
Killdeer, 35
King Eider, 20

**L**

*Lanius collurio*, 78
*Lanius meridionalis*, 78
*Lanius minor*, 78
*Lanius phoenicuroides*, 78
*Lanius senator*, 79
Lanner Falcon, 77
Lapland Longspur, 111
*Larus argentatus*, 49
*Larus cachinnans*, 50
*Larus canus*, 48
*Larus delawarensis*, 48
*Larus dominicanus*, 49
*Larus fuscus*, 50
*Larus glaucoides*, 49
*Larus hyperboreus*, 49
*Larus marinus*, 48
*Larus michahellis*, 50
*Larus smithsonianus*, 49
Laughing Dove, 115
Laughing Gull, 47
Leach's Storm Petrel, 58
*Leiothrix lutea*, 119
Lesser Black-backed Gull, 50
Lesser Crested Tern, 51
Lesser Flamingo, 116
Lesser Grey Shrike, 78
Lesser Kestrel, 76
Lesser Sand Plover, 35
Lesser Scaup, 20
Lesser Short-toed Lark, 84
Lesser Spotted Eagle, 68

Lesser Spotted Woodpecker, 75
Lesser Whitethroat, 92
Lesser Yellowlegs, 43
*Leucophaeus atricilla*, 47
*Leucophaeus pipixcan*, 47
*Limnodromus scolopaceus*, 41
*Limosa lapponica*, 37
*Limosa limosa*, 37
*Linaria cannabina*, 110
*Linaria flavirostris*, 110
Little Auk, 55
Little Bittern, 62
Little Bunting, 113
Little Bustard, 25
Little Crake, 28
Little Egret, 64
Little Grebe, 31
Little Gull, 47
Little Owl, 73
Little Ringed Plover, 35
Little Stint, 40
Little Swift, 25
Little Tern, 52
*Locustella luscinioides*, 91
*Locustella naevia*, 90
*Lonchura atricapilla*, 121
*Lonchura maja*, 122
*Lonchura punctulata*, 104
Long-billed Dowitcher, 41
Long-eared Owl, 73
Long-legged Buzzard, 72
Long-tailed Duck, 22
Long-tailed Jaeger, 55
Long-tailed Tit, 85
*Lophophanes cristatus*, 82
*Loxia curvirostra*, 110
*Lullula arborea*, 82
*Luscinia megarhynchos*, 98
*Luscinia svecica*, 98
*Lymnocryptes minimus*, 41

## M

Mallard, 18
Manx Shearwater, 59
Marbled Duck, 19
*Mareca americana*, 18
*Mareca penelope*, 17
*Mareca strepera*, 17

*Marmaronetta angustrirostris*, 19
Marsh Owl, 74
Marsh Sandpiper, 44
Meadow Pipit, 107
Mediterranean Gull, 48
*Melanitta fusca*, 21
*Melanitta nigra*, 21
*Melanitta perspicillata*, 21
*Melanocorypha calandra*, 84
Melodious Warbler, 90
*Melopsittacus undulatus*, 119
*Mergellus albellus*, 22
*Mergus merganser*, 22
*Mergus serrator*, 22
Merlin, 77
*Merops apiaster*, 74, 75
Mew Gull, 48
*Milvus migrans*, 71
*Milvus milvus*, 71
Mistle Thrush, 97
Monk Parakeet, 118
Montagu's Harrier, 71
*Monticola saxatilis*, 100
*Monticola solitarius*, 100
*Montifringilla nivalis*, 103
*Morus bassanus*, 61
*Motacilla alba*, 106
*Motacilla cinerea*, 106
*Motacilla citreola*, 106
*Motacilla flava*, 105
*Motacilla tschutschensis*, 105
Moussier's Redstart, 99
Moustached Warbler, 88
*Muscicapa striata*, 97
Muscovy Duck, 117
Mute Swan, 115
*Myiopsitta monachus*, 118

## N

*Neophron percnopterus*, 66
*Netta rufina*, 19
Northern Fulmar, 58
Northern Gannet, 61
Northern Goshawk, 70
Northern Harrier, 70
Northern Lapwing, 33
Northern Pintail, 18
Northern Raven, 81

Northern Shoveler, 17
Northern Wheatear, 101
*Nucifraga caryocatactes*, 80
*Numenius arquata*, 37
*Numenius hudsonicus*, 36
*Numenius phaeopus*, 36
*Numenius tenuirostris*, 36
*Numida meleagris*, 117
*Nycticorax nycticorax*, 63

## O

*Oceanites oceanicus*, 57
*Oceanodroma castro*, 57
*Oceanodroma leucorhoa*, 58
*Oceanodroma monorhis*, 58
*Oenanthe deserti*, 101
*Oenanthe hispanica*, 101
*Oenanthe isabellina*, 101
*Oenanthe leucopyga*, 102
*Oenanthe leucura*, 101
*Oenanthe oenanthe*, 101
Olive-backed Pipit, 107
*Onychoprion anaethetus*, 52
*Onychoprion fuscatus*, 52
Orange-breasted Waxbill, 121
Orange-cheeked Waxbill, 120
*Oriolus oriolus*, 79
Ortolan Bunting, 113
*Otis tarda*, 25
*Otus scops*, 72
*Oxyura jamaicensis*, 23
*Oxyura leucocephala*, 23

## P

Pacific Golden Plover, 34
Paddyfield Warbler, 89
*Pagophila eburnea*, 46
Pallas's Leaf Warbler, 87
Pallas's Reed Bunting, 114
Pallid Harrier, 71
Pallid Swift, 24
*Pandion haliaetus*, 65
Parasitic Jaeger, 55
*Parus major*, 82
*Passer domesticus*, 102
*Passer hispaniolensis*, 102

*Passer montanus*, 102
*Pastor roseus*, 95
Pectoral Sandpiper, 40
*Pelagodroma marina*, 57
*Pelecanus onocrotalus*, 116
*Perdix perdix*, 13
Peregrine Falcon, 77
*Periparus ater*, 81
*Pernis apivorus*, 66
*Petronia petronia*, 103
*Phaethon aethereus*, 56
*Phalacrocorax aristotelis*, 61
*Phalacrocorax carbo*, 61
*Phalaropus fulicarius*, 42
*Phalaropus lobatus*, 42
*Phalaropus tricolor*, 42
*Phasianus colchicus*, 117
*Phoeniconaias minor*, 116
*Phoenicopterus roseus*, 32
*Phoenicurus moussieri*, 99
*Phoenicurus ochruros*, 99
*Phoenicurus phoenicurus*, 99
*Phylloscopus bonelli*, 86
*Phylloscopus borealis*, 88
*Phylloscopus collybita*, 87
*Phylloscopus fuscatus*, 87
*Phylloscopus humei*, 86
*Phylloscopus ibericus*, 87
*Phylloscopus inornatus*, 86
*Phylloscopus proregulus*, 87
*Phylloscopus sibilatrix*, 86
*Phylloscopus trochilus*, 87
*Pica pica*, 80
*Picus sharpei*, 75
Pied Avocet, 33
Pied-billed Grebe, 31
Pink-footed Goose, 15
Pin-tailed Sandgrouse, 26
Pin-tailed Whydah, 104
*Platalea leucorodia*, 62
*Plectrophenax nivalis*, 112
*Plegadis falcinellus*, 62
*Ploceus cucullatus*, 120
*Ploceus melanocephalus*, 103
*Pluvialis apricaria*, 34
*Pluvialis dominica*, 34
*Pluvialis fulva*, 34
*Pluvialis squatarola*, 34
*Podiceps auritus*, 31

*Podiceps cristatus*, 31
*Podiceps nigricollis*, 32
*Podilymbus podiceps*, 31
*Poicephalus senegalus*, 118
Pomarine Jaeger, 54
*Porphyrio alleni*, 29
*Porphyrio martinica*, 29
*Porphyrio porphyrio*, 29
*Porzana carolina*, 29
*Porzana parva*, 28
*Porzana porzana*, 29
*Porzana pusilla*, 28
*Prunella collaris*, 105
*Prunella modularis*, 105
*Psittacula krameri*, 78
*Psittacus erithacus*, 118
*Pterocles alchata*, 26
*Pterocles orientalis*, 26
*Pterodroma deserta*, 58
*Ptyonoprogne rupestris*, 85
*Puffinus baroli*, 60
*Puffinus mauretanicus*, 59
*Puffinus puffinus*, 59
Purple Gallinule, 29
Purple Heron, 64
Purple Sandpiper, 39
*Pyrrhocorax pyrrhocorax*, 80
*Pyrrhula pyrrhula*, 109

# R

*Rallus aquaticus*, 28
Razorbill, 55
*Recurvirostra avosetta*, 33
Red Avadavat, 104
Red Crossbill, 110
Red Kite, 71
Red Knot, 38
Red Phalarope, 42
Red-backed Shrike, 78
Red-billed Chough, 80
Red-billed Leiothrix, 119
Red-billed Tropicbird, 56
Red-breasted Flycatcher, 99
Red-breasted Merganser, 22
Red-crested Pochard, 19
Red-eyed Vireo, 79
Red-flanked Bluetail, 98
Red-footed Booby, 61

Red-footed Falcon, 76
Red-knobbed Coot, 30
Red-legged Partridge, 13
Red-necked Nightjar, 23
Red-necked Phalarope, 42
Red-rumped Swallow, 85
Red-tailed Shrike, 78
Red-throated Loon, 56
Red-throated Pipit, 108
Redwing, 96
*Regulus ignicapilla*, 93
*Regulus regulus*, 93
*Remiz pendulinus*, 82
Richard's Pipit, 106
Ring Ouzel, 96
Ring-billed Gull, 48
Ring-necked Duck, 20
*Riparia riparia*, 84
*Rissa tridactyla*, 45
Rock Bunting, 112
Rock Dove, 27
Rock Sparrow, 103
Rook, 80
Roseate Tern, 52
Rose-ringed Parakeet, 78
Rosy Starling, 95
Royal Tern, 51
Ruddy Duck, 23
Ruddy Shelduck, 16
Ruddy Turnstone, 37
Ruff, 38
Rufous-tailed Scrub Robin, 97
Rüppell's Vulture, 67
Rustic Bunting, 113

# S

Sabine's Gull, 46
Saker Falcon, 77
Sand Martin, 84
Sanderling, 39
Sandwich Tern, 51
Sardinian Warbler, 93
Savi's Warbler, 91
*Saxicola maurus*, 100
*Saxicola rubetra*, 100
*Saxicola rubicola*, 100
Scaly-breasted Munia, 104
*Scolopax rusticola*, 41

Scopoli's Shearwater, 58
Sedge Warbler, 89
Semipalmated Sandpiper, 40
Senegal Parrot, 118
*Serinus serinus*, 111
Sharp-tailed Sandpiper, 38
Short-eared Owl, 73
Short-toed Snake Eagle, 68
Short-toed Treecreeper, 94
Siberian Stonechat, 100
*Sitta europaea*, 94
Slender-billed Curlew, 36
Slender-billed Gull, 46
Smew, 22
Snow Bunting, 112
Snow Goose, 14
Sociable Lapwing, 34
Solitary Sandpiper, 43
*Somateria mollissima*, 21
*Somateria spectabilis*, 20
Song Thrush, 97
Sooty Shearwater, 59
Sooty Tern, 52
Sora, 29
South Polar Skua, 54
Spanish Imperial Eagle, 69
Spanish Sparrow, 102
*Spatula clypeata*, 17
*Spatula discors*, 17
*Spatula querquedula*, 16
Spectacled Warbler, 93
*Spilopelia senegalensis*, 115
*Spinus spinus*, 111
Spotless Starling, 95
Spotted Crake, 29
Spotted Flycatcher, 97
Spotted Nutcracker, 80
Spotted Redshank, 44
Spotted Sandpiper, 43
Squacco Heron, 63
Steppe Eagle, 116
*Stercorarius longicaudus*, 55
*Stercorarius maccormicki*, 54
*Stercorarius parasiticus*, 55
*Stercorarius pomarinus*, 54
*Stercorarius skua*, 54
*Sterna dougallii*, 52
*Sterna forsteri*, 53
*Sterna hirundo*, 52

*Sterna paradisaea*, 53
*Sternula albifrons*, 52
Stilt Sandpiper, 38
Stock Dove, 27
*Streptopelia decaocto*, 28
*Streptopelia turtur*, 27
*Strix aluco*, 73
*Sturnus unicolor*, 95
*Sturnus vulgaris*, 95
Subalpine Warbler, 93
*Sula leucogaster*, 61
*Sula sula*, 61
Surf Scoter, 21
Swinhoe's Storm Petrel, 58
*Sylvia atricapilla*, 91
*Sylvia borin*, 91
*Sylvia cantillans*, 93
*Sylvia communis*, 92
*Sylvia conspicillata*, 93
*Sylvia curruca*, 92
*Sylvia hortensis*, 92
*Sylvia melanocephala*, 93
*Sylvia undata*, 92

# T

*Tachybaptus ruficollis*, 31
*Tachymarptis melba*, 24
*Tadorna ferruginea*, 16
*Tadorna tadorna*, 16
*Taeniopygia guttata*, 121
Taiga Bean Goose, 15
*Tarsiger cyanurus*, 98
Tawny Owl, 73
Tawny Pipit, 107
Temminck's Stint, 39
Terek Sandpiper, 42
*Tetrao urogallus*, 13
*Tetrax tetrax*, 25
*Thalassarche melanophris*, 57
*Thalasseus bengalensis*, 51
*Thalasseus maximus*, 51
*Thalasseus sandvicensis*, 51
*Thectocercus acuticaudatus*, 119
Thekla's Lark, 83
*Threskiornis aethiopicus*, 118
*Tichodroma muraria*, 94
Tree Pipit, 107
*Tringa erythropus*, 44

*Tringa flavipes*, 43
*Tringa glareola*, 44
*Tringa melanoleuca*, 45
*Tringa nebularia*, 45
*Tringa ochropus*, 43
*Tringa semipalmata*, 44
*Tringa solitaria*, 43
*Tringa stagnatilis*, 44
*Tringa totanus*, 44
*Troglodytes troglodytes*, 94
Trumpeter Finch, 109
Tufted Duck, 20
Tundra Bean Goose, 15
Tundra Swan, 15
*Turdus iliacus*, 96
*Turdus merula*, 96
*Turdus obscurus*, 96
*Turdus philomelos*, 97
*Turdus pilaris*, 96
*Turdus torquatus*, 96
*Turdus viscivorus*, 97
*Turnix sylvaticus*, 32
Twite, 110
*Tyto alba*, 72

## U

Upland Sandpiper, 36
*Upupa epops*, 74
*Uria aalge*, 55

## V

*Vanellus gregarius*, 34
*Vanellus vanellus*, 33
Velvet Scoter, 21
*Vidua macroura*, 104
Village Weaver, 120
*Vireo olivaceus*, 79

## W

Wallcreeper, 94
Wandering Albatross, 57
Water Pipit, 108
Water Rail, 28
Western Bonelli's Warbler, 86
Western Capercaillie, 13

Western Cattle Egret, 63
Western Jackdaw, 80
Western Marsh Harrier, 70
Western Olivaceous Warbler, 90
Western Orphean Warbler, 92
Western Osprey, 65
Western Reef Heron, 64
Western Swamphen, 29
Western Yellow Wagtail, 105
Whinchat, 100
Whiskered Tern, 53
White Stork, 60
White Wagtail, 106
White-backed Vulture, 66
White-crowned Wheatear, 102
White-faced Storm Petrel, 57
White-headed Duck, 23
White-headed Munia, 122
White-rumped Sandpiper, 40
White-rumped Swift, 25
White-tailed Eagle, 72
White-throated Dipper, 102
White-winged Snowfinch, 103
White-winged Tern, 53
Whooper Swan, 16
Willet, 44
Willow Warbler, 87
Wilson's Phalarope, 42
Wilson's Snipe, 42
Wilson's Storm Petrel, 57
Wood Sandpiper, 44
Wood Warbler, 86
Woodchat Shrike, 79
Woodlark, 82

## X

*Xema sabini*, 46
*Xenus cinereus*, 42

## Y

Yellow-breasted Bunting, 114
Yellow-browed Warbler, 86
Yellow-crowned Bishop, 103
Yellowhammer, 112
Yellow-legged Gull, 50

# Z

Zebra Finch, 121
Zitting Cisticola, 91

# Glossary of place names

The following list contains the names of the places mentioned in the text, along with a short description of their whereabouts. The most important ones, namely regions and capes, are included in the map presented on the following page (Figure 1).

Açude da Murta – a small reservoir close to the southern shore of the Sado estuary, about 10 km away from the coast

Albufeira lagoon – a coastal lagoon lying about 20 km south of Lisbon (known as 'Lagoa de Albufeira' in Portuguese) – not to be confused with Albufeira town in central Algarve

Alcácer do Sal – a small town in western Alentejo

Alcochete – a small town on the shore of the River Tagus, roughly 10 km from Lisbon

Alentejo – a large province in southern Portugal which covers almost all the territory south of the River Tagus, except the Algarve

Alentejo Litoral – the coastal part of the Alentejo province; it is about 50 km wide and extends from the Sado estuary southwards to the Algarve

Algarve – the southernmost province of Portugal, ranging from Cape St. Vincent in the west to Castro Marim in the east

Aljezur – a small town in the north-western part of the Algarve

Almada – a town on the southern bank of the River Tagus, just in front of Lisbon

Alqueva – a large reservoir in the eastern part of the Alentejo that has been constructed on the basin of the River Guadiana; it is one of the largest artificial lakes in Western Europe

Alto Alentejo – a former province corresponding to the northern half of the Alentejo (districts of Évora and Portalegre); nowadays this expression is used to refer to the Portalegre district alone

Alto Minho – the northern part of the Minho province, corresponding to the district of Viana do Castelo

139

**Figure 1 – Map of mainland Portugal showing the traditional provinces, the capital Lisbon and the most prominent capes**

Alto Rabagão – a large reservoir in northern Portugal, just east of Serra do Gerês; also known as Pisões reservoir

Anadia – a small town in the province of Beira Litoral, lying roughly midway between Coimbra and Aveiro

Ave – a river in northern Portugal, which reaches the sea at Vila do Conde, slightly to the north of Porto

Aveiro – a coastal town, lying roughly 50 km south of Porto, close to the mouth of the River Vouga

Azambuja – a small town close to the River Tagus, about 50 km northeast of Lisbon

Baixo Alentejo – the southern part of the Alentejo, corresponding to the district of Beja, with the exception of the county of Odemira, which is part of the Alentejo Litoral

Barão de São João – a village lying west of Lagos, in the western Algarve

Barra – a beach lying just west of Aveiro

Barragem de Santa Luzia – a very remote dam in central Portugal, lying near the small town of Pampilhosa da Serra, roughly midway between Coimbra and Castelo Branco

Barranco do Velho – a village lying in the hills of central Algarve, in Loulé county

Barrinha de Esmoriz – a small coastal wetland just south of Porto

Barroso – a region in extreme northern Portugal, lying east of Serra do Gerês

Beira Alta – a province in eastern Portugal, which ranges from Serra da Estrela north to the River Douro; its main towns are Guarda and Viseu

Beira Baixa – a province in eastern Portugal, which extends from Serra da Estrela south to the River Tagus; its main town is Castelo Branco

Beira Interior – literally 'inner Beira', this expression is used to refer to the whole of Beira Alta and Beira Baixa

Beira Litoral – literally 'coastal Beira', this province forms the coastal half of central Portugal; its main towns are Aveiro, Coimbra and Leiria

Beja – the main town in the southern part of the Alentejo, lying about 100 km north of the Algarve

Berlengas – a small archipelago lying about 10 km off the Portuguese west coast, near the town of Peniche

Boliqueime – a village in central Algarve, just north of Vilamoura

Boquilobo marsh – a small freshwater wetland close to the River Tagus, not far from Torres Novas, about 100 km northeast of Lisbon

Caldas da Rainha – a town in western Portugal, about 80 km north of Lisbon

Cape Carvoeiro – a prominent cape in western Portugal, just west of Peniche (about 80 km north of Lisbon)

Cape Espichel – a headland about 30 km south of Lisbon, just west of Serra da Arrábida

Cape Raso – a small cape lying about 25 km west of Lisbon

Cape Roca – a headland which forms the westernmost tip of the European mainland; it lies slightly to the north of Cape Raso

Cape Sardão – a cape in the coast of Alentejo, lying about 40 km south of Sines

Cape St. Vincent – forms the southwestern tip of the Iberian Peninsula, this is the place where Portugal's south and west coasts meet

Cascais – a coastal town lying about 20 km west of Lisbon

Castro Marim – a small town in the eastern Algarve, near the mouth of the River Guadiana; it is also the name of a small nature reserve nearby

Castro Verde – a small town in the Baixo Alentejo, which lies in the middle of the plains

Cávado – a river in northern Portugal, which has its source in the Barroso region and flows southwestwards, reaching the sea at Esposende, about 40 km north of Porto, where it forms a small estuary

Coimbra – an important town in central Portugal, it is the capital of the Beira Litoral

Douro – one of the major rivers in Iberia, it has its source in Spain and enters Portugal in its northeasternmost corner, at Miranda do Douro, reaching the sea at Porto

Douro Litoral – a small but heavily populated province in the north-western part of the country, its main city is Porto

Dunas de São Jacinto – a small nature reserve, lying close to the coastal town of Aveiro, in central Portugal; the place is best known as a waterfowl refuge

Dunas Douradas beach – a small beach just west of Quinta do Lago, in central Algarve

EEZ – see Exclusive Economic Zone

Elvas – a town lying in the eastern Alentejo, very close to the Spanish city of Badajoz

Escaroupim – a village in the Ribatejo province, on the shore of the River Tagus

Estarreja – a small town lying on the eastern side of Ria de Aveiro

Estoril – a small coastal town in the outskirts of Lisbon, lying about 20 km west of the capital, close to Cascais

Estremadura – this province lies in western Portugal and includes the Lisbon region; it extends as far north as Cape Carvoeiro and as far south as Setúbal

Évora – a town in central Alentejo

Exclusive Economic Zone – an area of sea stretching from the coastline out to 200 nautical miles from the coast.

Ferreira do Alentejo – a small town in the province of Baixo Alentejo, slightly west of its main town, Beja

Fuseta – a coastal village in the eastern Algarve, about 20 km east of Faro

Grândola – a small town in western Alentejo

Guadiana – one of the three largest catchments in the country; it runs westwards from Spain and turns south as it approaches Portugal; it reaches the sea near Castro Marim

Guadramil – a small village in the eastern part of Serra de Montesinho, close to Bragança

Guarda – a town in the Beira Alta province, which is also capital of a district

Ilha da Morraceira – a small island in the middle of the Mondego estuary, near the town of Figueira da Foz

International Douro – this is the name given to the stretch of the River Douro where it forms the border with Spain; it lies in the far northeast of Portugal

International Tagus – an area in eastern Portugal, about 50 km long, where the River Tagus forms the natural border with neighbouring Spain

Lagoa – a coastal town in the western Algarve, about 50 km west of Faro

Lagoa dos Patos – although it is known as Lagoa (Portuguese for 'lagoon'), this is actually a reservoir; it lies in the middle of the Alentejo, about 30 km northwest of Beja

Lagos – a coastal town in the western Algarve, about 70 km west of Faro

Lezíria Norte – a very flat area lying along the left bank of the River Tagus, roughly 30 km northeast of Lisbon

Lisbon – Portugal's capital and largest city, lying near the west coast and close to the Tagus estuary

Ludo – a farm in Ria Formosa, which lies just northwest of Faro airport

Manteigas – a small town in the heart of Serra da Estrela

Marvão – a small and old village in the northern Alentejo lying on top of a rock at nearly 900m altitude

Mexilhoeira Grande – a village near the Ria de Alvor, in the western Algarve

Mindelo – a small village not far from Vila do Conde, near the mouth of the River Ave

Minho (province) – lying in the north-western corner of the country, this province is the greenest in the whole country; its main city is Braga

Minho (river) – this river forms the border with Spanish Galicia in the north-western part of the country

Miranda do Douro – a very remote small town in the extreme northeast of Portugal, is part of an area known as International Douro

Mondego – the longest river in central Portugal, its source lies in Serra da Estrela and it flows westwards, passing Coimbra and entering the sea at Figueira da Foz, about 100 km south of Porto

Montemor-o-Novo – a small town in the western part of the Alentejo, lying about 100 km east of Lisbon

Mourão – a small town in the eastern Alentejo, 50 km east of Évora

Murtosa – a small town in the vicinity of Aveiro

Nazaré – a coastal town in central Portugal, lying about 100 km north of Lisbon

Óbidos lagoon – a coastal lagoon in central Portugal, roughly 80 km north of Lisbon

Odemira – a small town in southwestern Alentejo

Ovar – a small town in western Portugal, about 30 km south of Porto

Peniche – a coastal fishing town which lies close to Cape Carvoeiro and the Berlengas islands.

Pinhal Interior – an inland area in central Portugal, lying between the towns of Coimbra and Castelo Branco

Ponta da Almádena – a cliff west of Lagos, in the western Algarve

Ponta da Atalaia – a cliff on the southwest coast, about 40 km north of Cape St. Vincent

Ponta da Piedade – a large cliff close to the town of Lagos, in the western Algarve

Portas de Ródão – literally meaning 'doors of the Ródão'; this is a towering bottleneck in the River Tagus, not far from the Spanish border

Porto – the second largest town in the country, sometimes called the 'capital of the north'; it lies in the province of Douro Litoral

Porto de Mós – a small town in western Portugal, about 100 km north of Lisbon

Póvoa de Varzim – a coastal town in northern Portugal, about 30 km north of Porto

Quinta do Lago – an expensive tourist resort in the central Algarve

Ria de Alvor – a small estuary in the western Algarve, lying between Portimão and Lagos

Ria de Aveiro – a popular name given to the broad estuary of the River Vouga, which lies around the town of Aveiro

Ria Formosa – this is the largest wetland in the Algarve, extending over much of the central and eastern Algarve; the widest area lies around Faro

Ribacoa – a plateau lying in the Beira Alta province, between the River Coa and the Spanish border

Ribatejo – literally meaning 'on the shore of the Tagus', this province is mostly flat and comprises most of the lower Tagus valley, just northeast of Lisbon; the main town is Santarém

Ribeira de Alcantarilha - a tiny estuary lying just to the west of Salgados lagoon, close to Armação de Pera

Sado – a river in southern Portugal, which has its source in the southwest and flows northwards, forming a broad estuary and reaching the sea at Setúbal, near Serra da Arrábida

Sagres – a village near Cape St. Vincent, in the western Algarve, near the southwesternmost point in the country

Salgados lagoon – a coastal lagoon in the Algarve, (known as 'Lagoa dos Salgados' in Portuguese)

Santa Luzia (salt pans) – a complex of salt pans near Tavira, eastern Algarve

Santo André lagoon – the largest coastal lagoon in the country, lying on the southwest coast, about midway between Lisbon and the Algarve

São Cristóvão – a village in the Alentejo lying about 40 km west of Évora

Serra da Arrábida – a limestone chain of hills lying about 40 km south of Lisbon

Serra da Estrela – forms the highest peak in mainland Portugal and is part of Beira Alta and Beira Baixa

Serra de Monchique – a chain of hills in the western Algarve, rising to about 900m

Serra de Montesinho – a chain of hills lying in the extreme northeast of Portugal

Serra de São Mamede – a range of hills in Alto Alentejo, rising up to 1025m, thus forming the highest peak south of the River Tagus

Serra do Açor – a hilly area rising to about 1400m lying slightly to the southwest of the Serra da Estrela

Serra do Alvão – this Serra lies in the Trás-os-Montes province, near the town of Vila Real

Serra do Gerês – a mountainous area in north-western Portugal, which is home to the only national park in the country; it rises up to 1500m

Serra do Marão – an important Serra in northern Portugal which separates the western province of Douro Litoral from the north-eastern province of Trás-os-Montes

Serra dos Candeeiros – a hilly area in western Portugal, consisting mainly of limestone

Sesimbra – a small town lying at the southern tip of the Setúbal peninsula, just to the west of Serra da Arrábida

Setúbal – an important city lying about 40 km south of Lisbon, between Serra da Arrábida and the Sado estuary

Silves – an old town in the western Algarve, just north of Lagoa

Sines – a coastal fishing town, which lies on the west coast midway between Lisbon and the Algarve

Sintra – a charming small town lying just west of Lisbon, which also gives its name to the nearby range of hills

Sizandro – a small river in western Portugal, which forms a very small estuary roughly 30 km south of Cape Carvoeiro

Sorraia – a tributary of the River Tagus

Tagus – the longest river in the Iberian Peninsula, which has its source in Spain and flows westwards; it enters Portugal east of Castelo Branco, forming the so-called International Tagus and reaches the sea near Lisbon

Taipal marsh – a wetland area close to the River Mondego, about 20 km west of Coimbra

Tavira – a medium-sized town in the eastern Algarve

Terra Fria – a popular name which means 'cold land' and refers to the northern part of Trás-os-Montes province (roughly the area around Bragança and Miranda do Douro)

Tornada marsh – a small wetland lying near Caldas da Rainha, about 80 km north of Lisbon

Trás-os-Montes – the northeasternmost province of Portugal; important towns in this region are Bragança and Vila Real

Venda Nova – a large dam in northern Portugal, close to the Serra do Gerês

Viana do Castelo – a coastal city in northern Portugal, bordered by the River Lima and lying about 50 km north of Porto

Vila do Bispo – a small town near the southwesternmost tip of Portugal, in the western Algarve

Vila Franca de Xira – a town lying about 25 km north of Lisbon, on the right bank of the River Tagus

Vilamoura – a well-known luxury tourist resort in central Algarve, not far from Quinta do Lago

Vila Nova de Milfontes – a small coastal town in southern Portugal lying at the mouth of the River Mira, roughly 30 km south of Sines

Vila Real de Santo António – a town in the Algarve lying at the south-eastern tip of Portugal, near the mouth of the River Guadiana

Vouga – a river in central Portugal which flows westwards and meets the sea near Aveiro

# About the author

Gonçalo Elias was born in Lisbon, Portugal, in 1968. He started watching birds seriously in December 1987. He has wide-ranging field experience and a good knowledge of Portugal's territory, having visited all the counties in the mainland and almost all the islands. He has also explored over 30 different countries in four continents, in order to watch birds and has taken part in nine ornithological atlas projects in Portugal, Spain and Tanzania. He has authored or co-authored twenty books about the Portuguese birds and the best places to watch them, including: *Guia das Aves de Lisboa, As Aves do Estuário do Tejo, As Aves do Estuário do Sado, A Birdwatcher's Guide to Portugal, Aves de Portugal – Ornitologia do território continental, Aves de Portugal – Lista Anotada, Aves do Alentejo* and *Birding hotspots in the Algarve* (a series of eight books), along with several papers and notes in specialized journals. He is a founding member of SPEA – Sociedade Portuguesa para o Estudo das Aves, and was a member of the board between 1999 and 2002. He was the coordinator of the PRC – Portuguese Rarities Committee between 2002 and 2006. Since 2007 he has been actively promoting birdwatching using the new information and communication technologies; he is a founding member and administrator of Forum Aves (the largest online community of birdwatchers in Portugal), which was launched in July 2007, and also a founding member and coordinator of the avesdeportugal.info website, launched in January 2008. Within the scope of this website, he has been organizing, since 2011, free online courses, aiming at promoting skills in identification of the wild birds occurring in Portugal.

He has a degree in Electrotechnical and Computer Engineering (IST, 1991) and has an MBA (UNL, 1996); additionally, he is a professional trainer, certified by the IEFP.

CPSIA information can be obtained
at www.ICGtesting.com
Printed in the USA
BVHW031918170322
631787BV00004B/155

9 781658 662222